the raw food kitchen book

Amanda Brocket is a qualified raw food chef, teacher and coach. The Raw Food Kitchen Head Office is based in Sydney, and runs regular classes, retreats, offers raw food e-books and transformation programmes online, on the website therawfoodkitchen.com.au.
The Raw Food Kitchen Book is Amanda's first cookbook.

the raw food kitchen book

Amanda Brocket

Photography by
Chris Chen

LANTERN

an imprint of
PENGUIN BOOKS

summer sensation, see page 51

contents

recipes

amanda's story

Hello! Welcome to the wonderful world of raw foods. I want to tell you my story: how The Raw Food Kitchen was born, and what brought me here today to bring this beautiful book to you.

I wasn't always an energetic, motivated, confident or healthy individual, and I will tell you why shortly, but to be here, writing about this to you in an Australian first – a raw bible with fab recipes – I am having to pinch myself just a little bit.

I was born in Timaru, a sleepy town in the South Island of New Zealand, and was brought up on standard fare: WeetBix and milk, toast and Vegemite. Mum was brilliant at roasting lamb and pork chops with mashed potato and an array of well-boiled vegetables. Yoghurt, cheese and crackers were snacks. Treats were doughnuts, chocolate and pavlova, and 50 cent lolly bags when we had pocket money. Growing up, I loved cooking and baking. I loved making creamy lasagnes, quiches, pasta bakes, apple pies and anything with ice-cream.

Whenever we got sick we went to the doctor. Ear infection? Antibiotics. Sore throat? Antibiotics. Cold and flu? Antibiotics. Period too heavy at the age of thirteen? Contraceptive pill. Thrush at fourteen? Take Canesten. Acne really bad? Doxycycline (another antibiotic).

Fast forward to my mid-twenties and I'm now in Sydney, working in the fast-paced environment of advertising agencies. We worked hard and played hard and that suited me just fine; I loved any excuse to get stuck into the white wine for Friday afternoon work drinks.

At this time in my life I'd just gone through a relationship break-up, had zero self-esteem and thought I could get that back by losing weight, so I was into low-fat everything: low-fat milk, Special K, black coffee, ham and cheese brown bread sandwiches for lunch, Lean Cuisine and low-fat yoghurt for dinner. My favourite fruits were bananas, strawberries and passionfruit. Vegies were usually thrown into a stir-fry as a side to the main event, meat.

I certainly lost weight, but boy was I unhealthy. My acne was getting worse, as was the burning in my stomach every time I ate something. I had constant nasal drip, and despite being slim I had a bloated stomach, and I wasn't going to the toilet – at all.

I wasn't sleeping; in fact by this stage my insomnia had lasted almost two years. I would wake up at 1 a.m., 3 a.m. and so on. Hormonally, my periods were all over the place and I had a heavy pain in my ovary (it turned out to be a cyst, which burst painfully one night). I would have bouts of eczema over my eye. I was tired, I had joint pain, I was in a constant brain fog and I couldn't remember anything or focus on getting a task done. And then there were the cravings; oh, the cravings – they were intense. Sugar, ice-cream, chocolate, toast with Vegemite at all hours, coffee. The cravings were driving me to buying tubs of ice-cream at ten o'clock at night!

Mentally I was depressed, angry; even suicidal on some days. I knew this wasn't me, and every time I went to the doctor he would write another script for drugs that masked the problems for a while or made me worse. When my doctor threw his hands up in the air, at a loss as to what to do with me, I knew it was time to explore some alternatives. This was the beginning of my diagnosis of Systemic Candida (see page 16) and a five-year healing journey.

It was a slight relief to get a label for my symptoms, but also, strangely, I felt shame and guilt and hid the diagnosis from my workmates and friends for a long time.

When I visited a naturopath, I was put on an anti-candida diet. Very strict: no wheat, no dairy, no sugar, no vinegar, no alcohol, no yeast, no MSG, no coffee, no chocolate, no processed foods, no cereal, no milk, no yoghurt, no pasta, no pizza, no ice-cream, no cheese, no life!

There were supplements galore. Expensive ones, too. I took them religiously. The hardest thing for me to get my head around was the diet. I felt as if my life was over – all my comfort foods were being taken away from me; I was like a pouting toddler who has just had their favourite toy taken away. This was when I realised how addictive those foods were. If they could make me feel this bad because I couldn't have them, there must be a problem here!

But it still took me another year to really phase them out – I would eat them, knowing they were feeding my candida and would make me feel sick after every bite, but that's how addicted I was to them, and even when I managed to follow the anti-candida diet the cravings would taunt me.

During that time I was researching, researching, researching, exploring various treatment protocols, diet and detox methods; some worked, some didn't. I will share the ones that worked for me with you here in this book.

I also started to accept my illness. Learning to accept it and see the positives of the journey allowed me to be open to being okay with my body and its failings, and the lessons it was trying to teach me. This was the universe giving me a tap on the shoulder to say, 'Hey, you can't continue to abuse your body that way without serious consequences. It's time to love, nurture and honour yourself.' I was learning very quickly that healing is an emotional journey as much as it is physical, and to truly heal, both areas have to be worked on.

But the biggest and most exciting breakthrough for me was when, during one of my many detox retreat excursions to find true healing, I discovered raw foods. To see my old friends – cereal with milk, pasta, pizza, cheesecake, chocolate and more, but instead of being harmful, they were healing – was a huge lightbulb moment for me. Here was a way of life free from addictive, inflammatory foods such as wheat, meat, dairy, refined sugar, coffee, chocolate, additives and preservatives. And there was no sense of deprivation whatsoever; I could still have 'treats'. And it was all being handed to me on a very delicious-looking plate.

From that day I decided this was it. I had to try it. I went raw for two months and within that time discovered the magical world of superfoods, fermented foods (lifesavers for the cravings), sea vegetables and an amazing way of preparing many traditional dishes but in a raw version.

I was unstoppable. By the end of the two months my skin had cleared up, and I had lost the bloat and the extra few kilos without even trying. I was sleeping through the night and was happy and confident, with boundless energy. And my candida was gone. I couldn't remember ever feeling this good. Not only was I physically back to my old self (actually, better than my old self), but emotionally my outlook on life, people, relationships and connections had completely changed.

I went from being someone who hated social situations, who felt insecure and that I couldn't trust anyone, to someone who relished meeting people, creating connections and seeing the good and endless possibilities in everyone.

Candida is a silent epidemic, and most sufferers don't even know they have it. There are so many symptoms that seem unrelated, and most people go through life accepting them as 'normal': gas and bloating, headaches, migraines, fatigue, food cravings, anxiety, brain fog, insomnia, acne, eczema, PMS, thrush, joint pain and more.

My illness had been masked for many years with topical applications and pharmaceutical drugs because of misdiagnosed symptoms. If I'd had the knowledge back then that I do now, the first thing I would have changed would be my diet. And second, my emotional connection to myself.

In this book you will find many recipes that have inspired and motivated me along my raw journey and I hope you feel the same excitement as I do when making these delicious recipes. My intention is for you to use my insights into true health and healing and to try what resonates with you. From what I've seen with people joining my online programs, or attending our workshops, retreats or coaching sessions, most people who switch to a raw diet experience weight loss, increased energy, better sleep and better moods, at the very least.

For those of you who are suffering from candida, diagnosed or undiagnosed, I look forward to being a part of your healing journey. In this book you will find the health and detox tips that helped heal me from systemic candida and of course, some absolutely delicious raw food recipes for you to try in your own kitchen (we have given low-GI and sugar free options on some of these so keep an eye out). I believe it's everyone's birthright to have optimal health, happiness, boundless energy and enthusiasm, every day in every way.

With that said, it is officially The Raw Food Kitchen's mission and vision to help people create rawsome energy for life. Let's get rawsome together!

Most people find that going 100 per cent raw can seem overwhelming and too challenging straight away; eating just 20% raw can make a difference. So here at The Raw Food Kitchen we always encourage you to start slowly and not be too dogmatic about diet. Everyone is unique and what works for one person may not work for another. So the best place to start is to experiment in your kitchen and in your body.

This is the exciting part: you get to try something different and creative in the kitchen, with new and exciting ways of preparing food. As you start to tune in to your body, the more raw you go, you will find that you naturally gravitate towards the foods that serve you, making you feel healthy on the inside and look fab on the outside. And the beauty of raw is there is no calorie counting or deprivation. You still get to have treats such as chocolate, cheesecake, pizza and pasta, just a much healthier version of them.

Putting stress on yourself by worrying about calorie counting with restrictive diets, and the sense of deprivation that kicks in when you are 'not allowed' to eat something, does not make for a sustainable, long-term healthy change. Start by slowly phasing out the coffee, wheat, meat, dairy and processed foods while you start to add in raw food meals and options to your diet, and you will most likely find you will naturally and easily lose weight. I've also added some cooked vegan options to this book to make the transition easier.

aloha yoga, see page 51

Start by introducing a few green smoothies or juices and go from there. Build on that with a few raw food meals a week and a few raw snacks and treats (great to have on hand in the freezer or fridge) so that when you feel like a treat or a snack your go-to is a much healthier option than something processed out of a packet.

Once you have perfected a few raw food recipes, start building on them again with some more recipes. As you go deeper into your journey, take the time to listen to your body. How do you feel after eating? How is your mood, your sleep? How do you feel upon waking? Your body will give you the answer.

Try a fermented or cultured food recipe. These will really help with the cravings you may have initially. They are also powerhouses of enzymes, good bacteria and vitamins. You will also find as you go more raw and your body becomes more alkaline, your food cravings will disappear.

You may also find that going 20 or 50 per cent raw works for you and your lifestyle. Others love to be about 80 per cent raw. 100 per cent raw is great for cleansing or detoxing for a short period, but most people find it too challenging to do long-term, purely because of the world we live in; with work, social engagements and relationships, trying to follow a 100 per cent raw diet can be isolating.

If you do experiment with being 100 per cent raw and feel you have reached the point where you want to be – that is, you're feeling and looking good, and niggly health issues have cleared up – you may find that 50–80 per cent raw is a great place to stay.

This still leaves room for being social and eating 'normal' food from time to time. As long as the foundation of your diet includes raw, you will be feeling the benefits.

Don't stress too much about having all the fancy equipment; I started with a good quality food processor and high-powered blender. I used a potato peeler to create my zucchini pasta and put the oven on low (below 50°C) with the door open to activate my nuts and create my gluten-free breads. They might not have been technically raw but it was a lot better than blasting them at 250°C, I'm sure! I did this for six months until I was ready to upgrade my equipment and buy a dehydrator.

Lastly, it's important to be 100 per cent committed to making your health your number one priority. You must feel it in your heart, mind, body and soul. You want to go raw so much you will do whatever it takes. If you feel some resistance coming up or that there might be some emotional blocks around going raw, explore that; get some coaching or support if need be. Physical healing is also emotional healing and the two go hand in hand. The more your mind, body and soul are aligned to making true changes, the more of a success your raw journey will be and your health and vitality will come along in leaps and bounds.

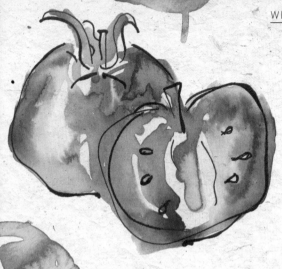

what does raw mean?

Raw foods or 'living foods' are foods in their whole form: unprocessed, fresh, and natural. They have not been refined, processed, heated over 44°C–48°C, denatured or altered in any way. Raw foods are as nature intended.

Why 44°C–48°C? This ensures the beneficial living enzymes in the food remain intact, and they actually give your body a helping hand in digesting food so you can easily assimilate all the wonderful nutrients, vitamins and minerals in them.

When you consume cooked foods, the body has to call on its own finite reserves of enzymes to digest them. If you have ever experienced that tired, sluggish feeling after eating a cooked meal, this is generally what's happening! It's a lot of work for the body. Because the enzymes in raw food help your body digest, they give it a break from all that work and time to turn its attention to 'cleaning house': clearing up dead cells and toxins, and essentially regenerating your body. This is primarily why raw foods are a very healing diet and most people experience renewed energy, more vigour, clearer skin, better moods and sleep, weight loss and more!

The term 'raw foods' for me not only means fruits, vegetables, nuts and seeds but also sea vegetables, gluten-free grains, superfoods, cold-pressed oils, sprouted foods and traditionally fermented foods.

A raw food diet is free from inflammatory foods such as wheat, gluten, refined sugar and dairy products. Anyone suffering from these food intolerances will love a raw food diet, and there is no deprivation as you won't be missing out on the much-loved foods you are used to eating, except this time, they are healing your body, not harming it. Yes, you still get to eat your pizza, pasta, cheese, ice-cream, cheesecake, milk and cereal, as well as chips and chocolate!

benefits of going raw

On a physical and emotional level you will most likely experience some or all of the following benefits: balanced hormones, improved strength, improved moods, clearer skin, better libido, renewed focus, energy and clarity, reversal of health problems, no bloat and weight loss.

Another great reason to go raw is sustainability and accountability. By choosing to switch to a mainly organic, plant-based diet, you are helping the planet.

It's no secret that dairy and meat farming is an intensive use of the land's resources. Natural forests are cleared to grow grain to feed animals for dairy farming, and natural lakes are being drained for irrigation. Then there is the run-off from dairy farms, which contributes to the pollution of our waterways. Large dairy farms treat animals as products, raised as quickly as possible using hormones, antibiotics and unnatural diets, and in some cases they are kept in crowded, confined conditions. Eating a mainly plant-based diet is compassionate and contributes towards creating a sustainable future for our planet.

If you do still choose to eat dairy, eggs and meat, please find your local farmers' market and get to know your farmer; ask how they raise their animals and care for them. Choose wisely; choose organic, free-range and grass-fed.

alkalise me!

Another amazing benefit of consuming a mainly plant-based diet is that it's very alkalising for the body. Why is this good for us?

Our blood cells like to be slightly alkaline to be healthy, and our bodies are in a natural homeostasis (healthy) state if we are slightly alkaline. Unfortunately for us, most of the foods we eat on the standard Australian diet and the lifestyle we lead today are acid-forming for the body. Fried foods, alcohol, coffee, artificial sweeteners, chocolate, wheat, dairy, meat, margarine, processed foods, canned foods, pasteurised foods and stress are big acidifiers.

For example, a can of Coke has a pH of 2! Extremely acidic. To buffer the acidity to protect our precious blood cells, the body will release a flood of alkaline minerals. If we don't have these freely available in our body, the body will literally pull minerals from our bones, perhaps one of the reasons why osteoporosis is so prevalant with today's modern diet.

If the body cannot eliminate the onslaught of acidity properly, this leads to toxicity, and an anaerobic (meaning without oxygen) environment in the body. Symptoms are wide and varied. Most of us have probably experienced the following: tiredness, bloating, weight gain, low moods, low energy, brain fog, cravings, candida, overgrowth of bad bacteria, parasites, shortness of breath, skin problems such as acne or eczema, headache, bad breath, insomnia, food intolerances, allergies or sinus problems.

In the long term, if toxicity or acidity are not addressed they can contribute to serious diseases such as diabetes, heart disease, lung, liver or kidney disease, auto-immune disease and cancer.

Most vegetables and fruits are alkalising in their raw form. Alkaline foods mean oxygenated bodily systems – the opposite of acidic or anaerobic systems. When the body is oxygenated internally, cells can function optimally, keeping the bad guys out and disease at bay.

I love to use the 80/20 rule here when consuming alkaline/acid foods: 80 per cent alkaline foods, 20 per cent acid foods. You could also use this rule when making smoothies; for example, 80 per cent greens, 20 per cent fruit or 20 per cent nuts. Or how about 80 per cent 'good' during the week, 20 per cent 'naughty'? This way you can still enjoy a social outing without feeling too stressed about what to eat or sticking to too many 'rules'. Raw foods should certainly form the basis or foundation of your diet or lifestyle, but being dogmatic about it can also create stress, if you're trying to do everything 'right'. Going raw should be a fun transition, one you can take at your own pace and that fits into your lifestyle as much as possible.

the protein/calcium/iron debate

A lot of people ask me, 'Where do you get your protein, iron and calcium from?' We have all been led to believe that the best sources of protein, iron and calcium come from meat. Not necessarily true! Most plants contain about 30–50 per cent protein, with hemp and spirulina having a whopping 50–70 per cent. Some of our favourite superfoods are also high in protein, such as chia, quinoa, nuts, seeds, goji, cacao, and bee pollen. If you are not strictly vegan you will want to know about bee pollen, as gram for gram it has 5–7 times more protein than meat. Plant-based protein is also more bio-available to the body than meat protein, because plants contain amino acids that help your body put together protein easily as opposed to a complete protein such as meat, which the body has to break down first to assimilate it.

Consuming about 7 per cent protein in our diet is more than enough. Current Australian government guidelines recommend that roughly 15–25% of your total energy intake per day is from protein. Their recommended sources of protein are meat, poultry, fish, eggs, dairy products, some grains and cereal-based products, beans, legumes, nuts and seeds (good to see nuts and seeds in here). The majority of the dairy and meat proteins are acid-forming in the body. If soy, beans and legumes are not prepared in the traditional way (soaked and/or fermented) and instead are heated and processed, they can cause digestive problems and act as mineral blockers in the body.

Most Australians consume far more protein than they need. Consuming excess protein can result in weight gain and stress on the kidneys, and it can cause minerals to leach from your bones. Excess protein gets converted to sugar and then fat. Increased blood sugar levels can feed pathogenic bacteria and yeasts such as candida.

It doesn't have to be all or nothing when it comes to choosing your protein sources. If you choose to eat meat, dairy products or other cooked, processed protein sources just ensure you are doing so in moderation, that it's organic, and you are combining it with a raw food meal of some sort that makes up the majority of your plate. This will help buffer the acidity and help your body with digestion. Don't forget also that when you are consuming a mainly plant-based diet and sourcing your protein requirements this way, you are also generally consuming low-GI foods, and getting your good fats, minerals, vitamins, antioxidants and beneficial enzymes in every bite!

HERE'S HOW YOU CAN EASILY GET OVER 15 MG OF IRON A DAY:

1/4 CUP SESAME SEEDS = 4.2 mg	1/2 CUP SPINACH = 3.2 mg
1/2 CUP QUINOA = 1.4 mg	1/4 CUP DRIED APRICOTS = 1.0 mg
1/2 CUP SWISS CHARD = 2.0 g	1 BEETROOT = .79 mg
1 SQUARE RAW CHOCOLATE = .5 mg	1 TEASPOON SPIRULINA = 3–5 mg

IRON

What is iron and why do we need it? Iron carries oxygen around our bodies. When you are low on iron, red blood cells are fewer and smaller, which means less oxygen for the body. You will start to feel low on energy and tired all the time.

Ironically (no pun intended), when I was a meat eater I was always anaemic. Since switching to a plant-based diet I have not had a problem with iron levels. My theory is as my body is functioning overall with more oxygen, and my uptake of vtiamins and minerals has increased, so too does my body's ability to efficiently uptake iron.

So where do you get your iron from? The average woman needs about 12–13 mg a day, while men need 16–18 mg and children 11–15 mg. You will find many plant sources that meet this need easily. Think cacao, nuts and seeds, flaxseeds, sesame seeds, vegetables, basil, tomato, silverbeet, watercress, spinach, and other leafy greens. Parsley is brilliant, as are seaweeds and some fruits such as apricots and prunes, figs and currants. Hemp seeds are a standout. Now that's real ironman food! It's important to note that soaking, blending or juicing your foods and combining them with vitamin C will really help increase the body's ability to absorb iron.

CALCIUM, VITAMIN D & B12

Again, another myth to debunk here. There is plenty of bio-available calcium in seeds, leafy greens, sea vegetables, brazil nuts, almonds, sunflower seeds and tahini, lemon zest, cinnamon, cabbage, basil, spinach, chives, parsley, ground oregano, broccoli, kale and seaweed. Dried prunes, dates and figs are also great. Twenty almonds have as much calcium as 60 ml of milk.

A daily dose of vitamin D also helps to strengthen bones, as does weight-bearing exercise. The best way for the body to absorb Vitamin D is through sun exposure, for about 10 minutes a day, outside peak UV times, on skin that does not have sunblock applied to it.

Raw vegans also get this question a lot: Where do you get your B12 from? B12 is important for nerve function and keeping blood cells healthy, and prevents you from feeling tired and weak. An interesting fact about B12 is that it's produced by bacteria. The general reason you may receive more B12 from an omnivorous diet than a plant-based diet is that cattle carry more B12 bacteria than plants do.

However, if you are low on stomach acid, have imbalanced gut flora, lack digestive enzymes or consume coffee, alcohol, drugs, antibiotics or the contraceptive pill, then even if you're a meat eater you won't be absorbing B12.

Studies have indicated that if a raw vegan diet is followed correctly, most vegans have more B12 in their systems than those of meat eaters. This is generally because raw vegans are healthier and have correct levels of digestive enzymes, stomach acid and gut flora. Sea vegetables also contain the bio-available form of B12 – another great reason to add these to your diet every day. Lastly, consuming traditionally fermented foods such as sauerkraut, kim chi and coconut kefir help the body produce B12 in the gut.

If you wish to supplement with B12, ensure you use a supplement that has the methylcobalamin B12, as it's purported to be better utilised and retained in the body than the hydroxycobalamin and cyanocobalamin versions.

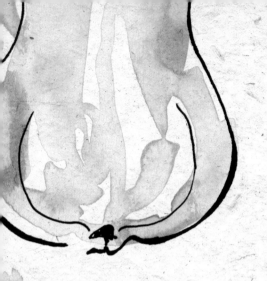

candida

Candida is a fungus that lives inside all of us, in harmony with our bodies and with the other bacteria that hang out in our mucous membranes, skin, mouths and bowels, and is usually kept in check by a healthy immune system.

Due to our modern diets and lifestyles, some health experts estimate that one in three people suffer from candida overgrowth and don't even know it. The symptoms can seem unrelated or mild, such as oral or vaginal thrush, or they can make you feel sick from head to toe.

Common symptoms of candida overgrowth are: gas, bloating, headaches, thrush, migraines, sinus problems, low energy, rectal itching, mood swings, constipation, anger, diarrhoea, acne, itchy body, sore throat, cough, strong body odour, food cravings, brain fog, chemical sensitivities, eczema, joint pain, indigestion, food intolerances, PMS, irregular periods, earaches, depression, insomnia, loss of libido, poor memory, and constant colds, flus and other illnesses.

Candida is also a very clever organism; it is a shapeshifter and can adapt to or tolerate many topical treatments, as well as live in harmony with certain other strains of good bacteria in the body. So what causes candida overgrowth? Antibiotics, the contraceptive pill, proton pump inhibitors or any drugs that suppress stomach acid production, your hormonal cycle, a depleted immune system, stress, an acidic diet (containing a lot of wheat, dairy, sugar, cooked foods, grains, alcohol, coffee and yeasts), steroids or a lack of good bacteria in the gut can all contribute.

HOW TO HEAL FROM CANDIDA

Outlined below is what worked for me, and in no way is this qualified medical advice, so always consult your naturopath to help you heal from your candida. It can be a long or short road to recovery, depending on the severity of your symptoms. Firstly, start with eliminating all sugar — that includes fruit sugar, dairy, refined grains, wheat, processed foods, alcohol, coffee, chocolate, vinegar, yeasts, and anything with added preservatives or flavours.

Add in lots of organic, raw vegetables – think colours of the rainbow, and include nuts, seeds and low-GI fruits such as lemons, grapefruit, limes, green apple or blueberries in small amounts (if tolerated – if not leave them out altogether). If your candida symptoms are severe, it's best to stay away from sweet vegetables such as carrot, beetroot and pumpkin.

Start eating traditional fermented foods every day: sauerkraut, coconut yoghurt or coconut kefir are great ones to start with. Use the recipes in this book to get you started.

Take high-dose probiotic capsules every day. Choose a product that has at least a 45 billion count and the more strains the better. Yoghurt and yoghurt drinks from the supermarket are not going to be your 'go-to' probiotic. They are not only loaded with sugar, preservatives and food additives, they have been heated at high temperatures, destroying most of the benefits of the good bacteria and making them acidic.

There are other great supplements out there that all help tame candida, such as clove oil, rosemary oil, oregano oil, olive leaf extract, pau d'arco (this makes a wonderful tea), garlic, coconut oil, apple cider vinegar, black walnut and neem oil.

Other products that may be worth exploring are those that contain the amino acid L-glutamine. This will help heal the gut and allow the body to establish a great foundation for healing overall. To support digestion during this time, digestive enzymes and betaine hydrochloric acid tablets will help your body digest food and limit fermentation in the gut – which candida loves to thrive in.

And lastly but most importantly, get those candida toxins out! Yes, this means colonics – lots of them – coffee enemas, infra-red saunas, intravenous vitamin C, liver support supplements, sweating, bentonite clay, meditation, yoga, green juices, high-quality filtered water and anything else that resonates with your body and helps it to heal.

Healing from candida requires a multi-pronged approach, as you can see. Once you start healing, symptoms may get worse before they get better, so if you start to feel tired or as if you have the flu, with achy joints, headaches or stomach upsets, or if you feel especially emotional during this time, try to welcome it; it's a sign your body is starting to heal, and trying to eliminate the dead candida cells. This is where getting colonics or booking a series of infra-red saunas will really help relieve those symptoms, and get you well faster.

gut health

If you suffer from gas and bloating you are not alone; most of us these days suffer some level of gas and bloating due to eating inflammatory foods, improper food combining, a poor diet, weak immune systems, weak gut walls and poor digestion. And to top it off, unhealthy bacteria and yeast thrive on sugar and carbohydrates, making you crave them and creating a vicious cycle.

If you suffer from headaches and feel tired all the time, you might want to look at what's going on in your gut. Bad bacteria produce toxic residues which damage the intestinal lining, and this is also a welcome mat for candida and parasites to make a home. Antibiotics, drugs, alcohol, sugar, wheat, dairy, refined and processed foods feed these guys too.

When levels of toxicity in the gut rise and start to enter the bloodstream, this blocks up our detox pathways and lowers oxygen in the body, and begins to show up as weight gain, mood swings, intolerances, skin issues, sleeping problems, energy depletion, hormonal imbalances, IBS and more.

Good bacteria help us with digestion. As food moves through our digestive tracts, good bacteria get to work on helping you digest food. They do this by producing digestive enzymes; particularly interesting to note is that they produce an enzyme called cellulase, which is required to digest fibre. If you're struggling to digest a diet high in fibre, you might want to consider showing some love to your good bacteria and increase your daily intake of them.

Good bacteria help to kill off pathogens and can help train the immune system to recognise both harmful pathogens and non-harmful antigens, therefore helping to prevent allergies. Good bacteria also help keep bad bacteria and yeasts such as candida in check.

Brain tissue and gut tissue develop from the same cells, which is why our gut is referred to as the second brain. A gut that is out of balance and contains too much bad bacteria or parasites can result in bad moods, mental disorders and depression.

WHY WE NEED TO OPTIMISE OUR INTAKE OF GOOD BACTERIA EVERY DAY

Our inner ecosystem needs to be diverse as all strains of good bacteria have a vital role to play in keeping us happy and healthy. Our modern lifestyles (stress, processed foods, alcohol) deplete our good bacteria. So a tub of yoghurt every day is not going to do it. Most yoghurt that you find in the supermarket has only a few strains, and has been heated at high temperatures, killing off most of the beneficial good bacteria and enzymes. So start to think of how many different ways you can get various strains into your body every day – the higher the count, the better. One of the reasons I am such a fan of traditional fermented foods is that they have good bacteria counts in the trillions and also offer a whole host of other beneficial enzymes, helping your body digest protein, fat and carbohydrates, and produce vitamins and fatty acids. They detoxify your body and help keep the gut wall strong. It's impossible for good bacteria to thrive in a toxic terrain. I believe that the best way to get your gut health regime off to a good start is to book a series of colonics. This will remove toxic build-up in the intestinal tract and create a nice clean home for the good bacteria to live in and thrive.

detoxing

Detox is a bit of a buzzword these days, and rightly so. We are living in a world where man-made pollution is at an all-time high; thousands and thousands of chemicals have been introduced to our environment since the 1700s. Our bodies have not evolved to effectively deal with and eliminate these toxins and chemicals in the air, water and soil, in the food we eat, plastics, our clothes, cars, household products and furnishings. Our bodies also have to process our own toxins, a by-product of our metabolism. When our bodies are tired, low on energy, depleted of nutrients, overburdened with toxins, or imbalanced in general, our detox pathways are not going to work efficiently.

I also believe that when our bodies are overworked trying to process toxins and can't manage to do this efficiently, they will send them to our fat cells for storage. This is the safest place for the body to store toxins, as they are stowed away from vital organs. Not good for our waistlines, though.

Switching to a raw food diet, eating clean and giving your body a break gives it the signal to start removing toxins; this is why most people experience easy weight loss when switching to raw. The toxins are literally dissolving from our fat cells.

When detoxing happens, depending on the person and how quickly they have made a change in their diet, detox reactions can occur when the body is dumping toxins faster than it can eliminate them. These can show up as tiredness, fatigue, low energy, upset stomach, bloating, nausea, flu-like symptoms, worsening of existing or pre-existing health conditions, skin conditions, anger, sadness, irritability, constipation, diarrhoea, joint and muscle pain, headaches, or even migraines.

To help ease detox reactions, I believe booking a series of colonics is essential (we'll talk more about that topic later), as is doubling your intake of high-quality filtered water, and sweating – infra-red saunas are great for this as they target organs deeply, helping remove toxins through the skin. Easing into a raw food diet slowly will also help minimise detox reactions.

Lastly, it's a good idea to rest as much as possible while you detox. The body is working hard on healing, so give it plenty of time and space to allow it to focus on doing just that. Being kind to yourself, easing off on the exercise but incorporating gentle walking to keep the lymph system moving is a good idea, and so is one of my favourite feel-goods at any time – getting a massage! This will also help move toxins out of the muscles into the lymph system.

However, some of you (me included) like to welcome these detox symptoms. It's a sign our bodies are pushing out the junk to make way for a more oxygenated, healthier system.

So despite feeling ick, get a little excited about the wonderful innate healing ability our bodies have once given the right signals and environment. However, if those toxins aren't removed, guess what happens? That's right, the toxins get re-absorbed into your body. What a double whammy. Hello colonics!

why I love colonics

Anyone who comes to my workshops or retreats knows that I love to talk about colonics. Why? During my healing journey with systemic candida, as I tried many different diets and supplements, I would go through various detox reactions. I just felt worse and worse. So I would blame what I was doing and go back to my normal diet and lifestyle to stop the reactions. Big mistake. The reason I wasn't getting better was because I was not removing the toxins from my body! Enter colonics.

Colonic irrigation has been around since the dawn of time, and was popular in Egyptian, Chinese, Hindu, Greek and Roman cultures. J.H. Kellogg (of Kellogg's cereal fame), a skilled physician and surgeon, was a huge advocate of colonics. He reported in the Journal of the American Medical Association in 1917 that he was able to successfully treat all but 20 of 40 000 gastrointestinal patients using only diet, exercise and enemas – no surgery.

Colonics work by introducing clean filtered water into the colon; this is done slowly and then held for a short period of time and released. It's all done through a small tube, and there is no mess or smell. Think of it like a washing machine soak cycle: it's soaking and softening all the toxic build-up and mucus off the colon walls, and then the rinse cycle removes the waste and toxins that have accumulated over the years from the colon wall.

Depending on how toxic your body is, you may need a series of treatments to really start to feel great. Colonics are hydrating for the body as well as stimulating reflex points in the colon, leaving you with a general feeling of wellbeing all over. Having a clean colon, and introducing good bacteria afterwards (such as a good probiotic capsule or fermented food or drink) allows the good bacteria to colonise, and then feeding it food that it loves – fresh, clean, raw foods (prebiotics) – allows the colony to really take hold and grow, granting the body balanced gut flora, a flat tummy and a happy mind.

It's super important, with your newfound energy and health, to make 'detox maintenance' part of your daily, weekly and monthly routine. Just as brushing your teeth is a daily habit you carry out, almost without thinking about it, so should be your detox routine. Eating clean as much as possible, exercise, and including infra-red saunas (do an internet search for one in your local area) as part of your regular life is a great place to start. Find a good colonic hydrotherapist in your area (also see page 234) and they will work with you and advise you on a treatment plan based on where you are on your health journey.

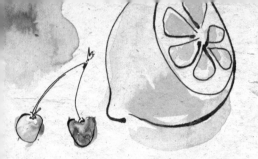

planning and prepping for raw

Making raw foods a part of your lifestyle does take a little bit of extra time and a change of mindset in the way you plan and prepare meals. You may find initially that it takes a lot longer to make a salad, or find it frustrating that a pizza in the dehydrator needs to be in there for over eight hours.

But as you get used to being a little more organised and using different processes to prepare meals, and have perfected a few recipes, everything gets quicker and you settle into a routine as new habits become second nature. I'm going to share my top tips with you for making raw foods easy in the kitchen.

MAKE A MEAL PLAN AND SHOPPING LIST

Roughly plan what you are going to eat each week. Allow a few free meal days so you have the flexibility to eat out. This doesn't mean a free pass to the local fast food joint, though. It still means choosing a healthy option if you're out, and making sure there is something raw featured on the plate if possible.

Then write down all the ingredients you are going to buy when you shop. You may find that the grocery bill is initially higher while you get your pantry staples organised, but once you have them you will probably find the grocery bills are about the same, as you have cut out meat and dairy.

SHOPPING

While we encourage you to go organic, the cost can be prohibitive for some people. A nice compromise is to go organic with some of the more usually heavily sprayed fruits and vegetables, such as stone fruits, berries and leafy greens, and buy the rest as conventional produce.

Farmers' markets are a great way to save money on organic produce; it's fresher and you get to meet the people who grow it, or who know their suppliers and take pride in what they offer. Google to find out about your local markets and make a date to go. There are also great online stores now where you can order online and have fresh produce delivered to your door. And find somewhere you can bulk-buy your nuts and seeds. This is much cheaper than buying them pre-packaged.

TIME-SAVER SECRETS

When you get home from your shop, start soaking all your nuts and seeds and anything you want to sprout at once. Make a note of their soaking times so you know when to drain and rinse them. For example, almonds need eight to ten hours, so a great habit to get into is to pop them in a bowl before you go to bed, then drain and rinse in the morning. Once your nuts and seeds have drained, you can either put some in the fridge in an airtight container to use to make sauces, turn into cereals or other meals, or eat them as they are. They are delicious this way and will last about five days in the fridge.

Alternatively, you can bag up your soaked nuts and seeds and pop them in the freezer, ready to make nut milk whenever you need it, or pop them in the dehydrator to dry out; they will keep for months if done this way. Or bulk-soak and dehydrate a whole range of nuts so they are always on hand for when you need them.

Your sprouts will need a few days of draining and rinsing, but by mid-week you can use these to turn into delicious salad toppers, eat them on crackers or a throw them into a raw cereal (think buckwheat, quinoa) that comes out super crunchy if put in a dehydrator!

When doing your meal plan, if it includes some dehydrated raw meals, plan to have them at the end of the week, as this way you have the time to prep them and have them drying in the first few days of the week, ready to eat a few days later.

Once your dehydrated food is done, you can eat it straight away or store it for later use. Think crackers, pizza bases, breads, raw cereals, nut cheeses, kale chips, nachos, quiches and more. Dehydrating food is a way to preserve it, so foods will have a longer shelf life after being in the dehydrator. Just make sure they are well sealed. I like to use mason jars for storing crackers, nuts and snacks. No more plastic and they look pretty.

During the first half of the week time savers could be more fresh, easy recipes, using the soaked nuts you have in the fridge to make a few different raw dressings. Raw dressings also last about a week in the fridge.

Set aside some time on Sunday afternoon to make some sauerkraut or a low-GI sweet treat you can pop in the fridge or freezer to have on hand during the week. This way you always have some healthy go-to options for when the munchies strike.

Once you start to get into this routine, creating delicious raw meals will become second nature. Another great motivator to keep going is how amazing you will feel just from eating this way!

specialist ingredients

We use a lot of unique ingredients in raw food preparation, and most of these are readily available in good health food stores, or select supermarkets. If you can't find them in a shop, try online. Here's a handy run-down to demystify them for you, and how to use them.

BINDERS AND THICKENERS

Chia seeds are not only an amazing superfood in their own right, these tiny seeds also make great binders, as when soaked they can absorb ten times their own weight in water. Great for crackers, chia porridge, desserts and pie crusts, either ground or whole in your smoothies, dressings, soups or sauces.

Flaxseeds (also called linseeds) are super high in fibre, and are a great source of micronutrients, magnesium, vitamin B1, and omega 3 fatty acids. They are rich in plant lignans, which can help regulate hormones and protect against breast cancer. Great for making crackers with or when ground, can be added to other recipes to make desserts or breads.

Irish moss is actually a seaweed that expands to more than double its volume when soaked. It is either then added to recipes as is or blended to make a gel, which you can use to thicken smoothies, sauces or desserts – think chocolate mousse! In its whole raw form, it's rich in trace minerals and vitamins, lowers inflammation, and soothes the gastrointestinal tract. You can purchase it online or from larger health food shops.

To make Irish moss paste, rinse a handful of moss to remove any remaining sand. Soak for 4–24 hours in filtered water at room temperature, rinsing a few more times. The moss will double in volume and feel slippery and soft. Don't worry if there is a faint moss smell – it will be odourless and tasteless at the end of the process. Place the moss in a high-powered blender and blend with enough filtered water to make a paste. Store it in the fridge for 2–3 weeks and use as needed. If unavailable, Irish moss paste can be replaced with the same quantity of melted coconut oil, but you won't get the same spongy texture as you would from the moss.

Psyllium is the husk of the plantago herb seed. It makes a great binder, as it contains a spongy fibre that can soak up a lot of water. Also used for weight control and for general intestinal health. Reduces appetite, improves digestion and cleanses the system. Every 100 grams of psyllium provides 71 grams of soluble fibre. Use in desserts, breads, crackers and wraps.

FERMENTED FOODS

I love fermented foods. These should become a staple in your diet every day for optimal gut, immune and brain function. Add sauerkraut as a condiment with any meal, eat it on a cracker mixed with avocado, or have kombucha or coconut kefir shots as an aperitif before every meal!

Coconut kefir is simply coconut water fermented with a couple of high-count, broad-spectrum probiotics in a 1 litre Grolsch bottle (a glass bottle with a rubber seal), left out at room temperature for approximately 36 hours to ferment. Once fermented, it's fun to add some flavouring to it, such as vanilla bean pods, goji berries, or passionfruit, vanilla or coconut medicine flowers and pop in the fridge for a lovely, healthy, delicious drink.

Kombucha is a fermented, effervescent drink made from a SCOBY (symbiotic colony of bacteria and yeasts, also known as the 'mother'), tea and organic sugar. Kombucha is a very beneficial drink to have every day for an energy boost; it's rich in B vitamins, helps increase metabolism, relieves PMS, breaks down bad estrogen and supports detoxification.

Sauerkraut is a potent chelator (detoxifier), contains super-high levels of probiotics, and helps the good bacteria in your gut produce B, K2 and D vitamins, reduces risk of stroke, diabetes, obesity and cancer, and improves mood and skin conditions. Just 8–10 tablespoons of sauerkraut contain up to ten trillion good bacteria, more than a whole bottle of probiotic capsules.

GLUTEN-FREE GRAINS

Amaranth is a small, gluten-free, grain-like seed, which tastes lovely sprouted. Amaranth is high in minerals, vitamins, protein and fibre. Use in crackers, cereals, raw breads and savoury dishes.

Buckwheat is a grain-like seed, is low-GI and quite alkaline. It contains no gluten. Buckwheat has more protein than rice, wheat, millet or corn and is high in the essential amino acids lysine and arginine. Sprout buckwheat and use it raw to enhance its nutritional content and make it super easy to digest. Use in desserts as extra crunch in fillings or in quiche bases, toppings, or raw cereals.

Millet has a lovely creamy flavour, and is gluten-free and highly digestible. Millet is also quite alkalising for the body. High in magnesium and B vitamins, low-GI and contains prebiotics to feed your gut flora and keep you happy. Sprouted, it makes a wonderful addition to any salad, dessert, cereal or cracker.

Quinoa is another grain-like seed that is gluten free, and high in minerals and protein, as well as containing large amounts of flavonoids, including quercetin and kaempferol. These are potent plant antioxidants with numerous health benefits. Again, sprout quinoa when using it raw to enhance its nutritional profile and make it super-easy to digest. Use as a cous cous substitute, or add to salads, crackers, savoury dish bases and raw breads.

GOOD FATS

Use cold-pressed oils, as they retain their nutritional value, unlike oils that have been heated at high temperatures or otherwise processed, which destroys nutrients. At high temperatures, oils can also become toxic and cause inflammation in the body. Other processed oils can also be derived from GMO crops such as canola.

Not all fats are bad. Good fats are essential for optimal brain and cellular function; your body also uses them to make hormones and help it use vitamins.

Coconut oil contains lauric acid, caprylic acid and capric acid, which contain anti-fungal, antibacterial, antiviral properities to boost the immune system. Great for fighting candida and bad bacteria. Lauric acid contains the highest concentration of medium-chain fatty acids (MCFAs), which are a healthy form of saturated fat. Coconut oil is immediately converted into energy – fuel for the brain and muscles rather than being stored as fat; it actually helps boost your metabolism and your body's fat-burning ability. Coconut oil also has a high smoke point, so it's perfect for cooking with, as it will not turn toxic at high temperatures. It also imparts a wonderful flavour to all your meals. Coconut oil sets solid below 25°C. When working with coconut oil in raw food recipes, warm it up gently by popping the jar in a pot of hot water so it becomes liquid. Coconut oil helps set raw desserts and sweet treats, as well as imparting a lovely velvety consistency when added to smoothies and dressings.

Flaxseed oil is loaded with omega 3s, which reduce inflammation in the body, stabilise blood sugar and protect the heart. Flaxseeds are also rich in antioxidants, B vitamins, dietary fibre, a group of phytoestrogens called lignans, protein, potassium and magnesium, which help regulate hormones and protect against breast cancer.

Flaxseed oil, like hemp, can go rancid quickly so store it in an amber glass jar in the fridge at all times. Being cold pressed, it should not be heated. Use for salad dressings.

Hemp seed oil has been dubbed 'nature's most perfectly balanced oil', as it contains a balanced 3:1 ratio of omega 6 (linolei/LA) to omega 3 (alpha-linolenic/LNA) essential fatty acids, the optimum requirement for long-term healthy human nutrition. Hemp also contains other important essential fatty acids necessary for a healthy life. It is compused of about 35 per cent protein, in a very easy-to-digest form that contains globular edestin and albumin – soft, broad-spectrum proteins that are low-allergy, so it's a great alternative for people who have allergies to soy or whey protein. Hemp is a cold-pressed oil and has a low smoke point, so it should only be used for dressing salads or making sauces in a raw food diet. It can go rancid quite quickly, so always keep it in the fridge. It also has a strong grassy flavour, similar to that of extra virgin olive oil, so I like to use half hemp and half olive oil when making recipes with it.

A NOTE ON HEMP

At the time of writing this book Australia is the only country in the world to make human consumption of hemp illegal, due to its relation to the cannabis plant and its low (0.05) THC level, which does not have any psychoactive effects. I hope this outdated legislation will change soon, as hemp is an extremely sustainable crop that has many uses in body care, clothing, fabrics, paper, plastics, building materials and fuel, as well as producing seeds that have superfood status. Hemp does not require the use of pesticides or herbicides and is a natural weed suppressant. Hemp products can be purchased from health food shops as products to use on your body or feed to your pets.

NATURAL FLAVOUR ENHANCERS

Miso paste is a paste made from soy beans, brown rice, barley or other grains that have been fermented using a fungus called *Aspergillus oryzae*. It's teeming with beneficial enzymes, good bacteria, vitamins, minerals and protein, and helps with digestive problems as well as assisting the gut to manufacture vitamins. Use in dressings, sauces and soups. Just make sure to look for an unpasteurised brand and use it with warm rather than hot foods or liquids (as these will destroy the precious enzymes and good bacteria).

Nutritional yeast is a deactivated yeast, so it does not affect those with candida. It is a complete protein and gives raw vegan food a wonderful cheesy flavour, and is also high in B vitamins, particularly B12.

Tamari is a wheat-free version of soy sauce, and because it is fermented, much easier to digest. Tamari is rich in several minerals and a great source of B3, protein, manganese and tryptophan. Not technically raw, but adds a wonderful rich flavour to any dish due to the amino acids in the soy protein.

SALT

Celtic sea salt has very similar benefits to Himalayan crystal salt, but it is unrefined sea salt. Celtic sea salt has a slightly stronger flavour, so use sparingly.

Himalayan crystal salt contains all the eighty-four essential trace minerals our bodies need to function optimally. It helps balance electrolytes and is antibacterial. Use in everything to help bring out the flavour of a dish.

Murray River pink salt contains no additives or preservatives and is loaded with natural minerals and elements such as magnesium and calcium. These natural mineralised brines give the salt its pink colour, as well as a lovely flavour.

GOOD FATS (CONTINUED)

Olive oil should be purchased organic (as conventional olives can be heavily sprayed), and only used for raw main meals, salads or raw dressings. It has many wonderful medicinal qualities: natural olive oil contains 70 per cent monounsaturated fatty acid (MUFAs). As a result, it lowers cholesterol and reduces heart problems. It reduces LDL ('bad') cholesterol levels, while at the same time increasing HDL ('good') cholesterol levels. Some research shows that MUFAs may also benefit insulin levels and blood sugar control, which can be especially helpful if you have type 2 diabetes.

Sesame seed oil – Cold-pressed sesame seed oil is rich in calcium and high in omega-6 polyunsaturated fatty acids. It's also stable at room temperature, due to its natural preservatives sesamol and sesamin, and may help with many modern-day illnesses such as high blood pressure, high cholesterol and diabetes. It has high levels of vitamin E, and is also naturally antibacterial and antiviral, and helps lower inflammation. It has such a wonderful flavour and is great to use in Asian-inspired raw dishes, marinades and dressings.

SEA VEGETABLES

Arame comes dried in black strips and has a lovely mild flavour. Soaking it for 10 minutes gives it an al dente consistency, and it's great in salads or soups. It's alkalising, rich in essential trace minerals and chlorophyll.

Dulse comes dried and can be purchased in flakes. Makes a great salt substitute if you prefer not to use salt. It has a mild flavour, and is great sprinkled in salads or used in salad dressings for a wonderful subtle, salty, savoury flavour. It's rich in vitamins and minerals, especially iodine, and helps the body detoxify from heavy metals, as well as supporting healthy thyroid function.

Kelp is richer in iodine than some of the other seaweeds, as well as other minerals, and a lot stronger in flavour. It's great to add to miso soups or if you prefer, you can take it in tablet form once a day. Kelp has many wonderful benefits: it helps detoxify the body, protects against radiation, promotes healthy thyroid function and protects the heart.

Wakame is rich in vitamins and minerals, particularly magnesium, helps the body burn fat, helps prevent heart disease, cancer and diabetes, and is low in calories and a great antioxidant. Wakame is delicious soaked, marinated, drained and combined with salads or my favourite, added to a sauerkraut mix (as this will enhance all the nutritional benefits).

SUPERFOODS

Acai is the famous purple berry from the Amazon. Contains omega 3, 6 and 9 fatty acids, amino acids, a range of minerals and vitamins, and is rich in antioxidants. Reduces inflammation and improves cellular health. Great in smoothies, chia porridge, desserts and coconut yoghurts.

Bee pollen is very high in protein. It is considered one of nature's most complete foods; it is alkalising, high in vitamins, minerals, antioxidants and essential fatty acids. Very high in enzymes, so it helps with digestion. Great sprinkled over cereal or added to a smoothie, or can be eaten on its own.

Cacao is chocolate, but in its raw, unprocessed form. Because it has not been heated at high temperatures like cocoa, all its beneficial minerals and vitamins remain intact. It also contains feel-good chemicals such as tryptophan, serotonin and phenylethylamine, which is known as the 'love hormone'. Great source of iron, calcium and magnesium. Add to nut milk for a chocolate milkshake, throw into smoothies or use it to make your favourite raw dessert, brownie or chocolates.

Camu camu is a berry from the Amazon, available here as a powder in its raw form. It has 14 per cent vitamin C by weight, and as this is food-derived, is more readily absorbed by the body than a synthetic vitamin C supplement. Good for collagen, detoxing and the immune system. Has a tart flavour and is great with orange juice, or in smoothies. You can also take it on its own – 1 teaspoon in a glass of water.

Chia seeds are high in omega 3 fatty acids and fibre, and are a rich source of amino acids, contributing to their high protein content; they also contain antioxidants, calcium, vitamins and minerals. They are gluten-free, easily digestible, and reduce cravings. Sprinkle on salads or soak to make a chia porridge.

Chlorella is a single-cell green algae. Its high concentration of chlorophyll acts as an excellent heavy metal detoxifier for the blood. Chlorella is packed with beta carotene, vitamin B complex and B-12, magnesium, iron, RNA, DNA, protein and amino acids. Take it in capsule form during times of detoxification such as juice fasting. However, it's also great to throw into green smoothies or juices in powder form.

Goji berries support the adrenal glands and kidneys, and enhance strength, stamina and longevity. They also increase alkalinity in the body. Great in cereals, smoothies or salads.

Hemp seeds – See hemp seed oil entry under 'Fats' on page 28–9 for nutritional information.

Lucuma – see entry under 'Sweeteners' on page 34 for nutritional information.

Maca is a tuberous vegetable grown in the Andes. It helps increase blood oxygen, is an adaptogen, and has unique alkaloids to help balance the endocrine system – great for women, as it increases energy and libido! It has a malt-like flavour and pairs well with cacao, citrus, caramel and butterscotch flavours. Throw into smoothies, desserts, savoury dishes and sweet treats.

Maqui is a purple berry from Chile, available in powder form, which has extremely high anti-oxidant levels and is very high in anthocyanins. Anthocyanins (which give it that beautiful dark pigment) help inhibit the formation of blood clots involved in strokes, pulmonary embolisms and heart attacks, promote higher levels of 'good' cholesterol, help stop oxidation of bad cholesterol, lower inflammation in the body and neutralise free radicals. Pairs wonderfully well with blueberries and acai. Add to smoothies, desserts or sweet treats.

Medicinal mushrooms such as reishi, cordyceps, chaga, shiitake, lion's mane and maitake generally come in powdered or extract form and are a wonderful addition to smoothies or tonics. Paired with other superfoods, just one teaspoon or two a day is a great way to keep your immune system functioning optimally. Each of these mushrooms has unique benefits but they can all help heal and prevent a wide variety of illnesses, and are antibacterial and antiviral, and enhance energy and vitality. I like to use Ancient Wisdom, which combines medicinal reishi with adaptogenic herbs.

Mesquite - see entry under 'Sweeteners' on page 34 for nutritional information.

Spirulina is a freshwater-growing blue-green algae, rich in chlorophyll (a blood builder) and phycoyanin, a health-enhancing pigment which gives spirulina its blue tint. It's also 71 per cent protein, contains all the amino acids, and it's high in vitamins A, B1, B2, B6, E and K. Throw into your green smoothie in the morning, or take it on its own with some water.

SWEETENERS

Using primarily low-GI sweeteners in recipes helps keep blood sugar levels stable and avoids the nasty sugar high and crash that comes from consuming highly processed sugars. Anything over about 50 on the GI scale is considered high. Some of these sweeteners don't affect blood sugar levels at all, and are safe for people suffering from candida or diabetes. Here's a list of my favourites:

Coconut nectar has a GI of 35; when compared to cane sugar, which has a GI of 68, coconut nectar is the better choice. Coconut nectar also has a naturally high mineral content and contains potassium, magnesium, zinc and iron as well as vitamin B1, B2, B3 and B6. It's unfiltered and preservative-free. Coconut nectar is a great sweetener to use in your sauces, smoothies and desserts. Keep in the fridge once opened.

Lucuma is a fruit from South America that comes in powder form in Australia and is a low-GI superfood. It has a wonderful creamy citrus flavour that pairs well with other citrus and creamy fruits – think banana, mango, avocado, pear, orange, lemon, guava and passionfruit. Use it as a base in your smoothies, desserts or sweet treats. Lucuma is an excellent source of carbohydrates, fibre, vitamins and minerals. It has lots of beta-carotene, niacin (B3) and iron.

Maple syrup is available in various grades. There are also imitation maple syrups out there, so check the label and make sure it doesn't say 'maple syrup flavour'. Not technically raw, but a naturally occurring sugar with all its minerals still intact. Remember, the darker the syrup, the more antioxidants and stronger flavour it will have. Grade A is further categorised into three groups: light amber, medium amber and dark amber. Grade B is the darkest of them all.

Maple syrup has a GI of 54, so it is quite high in sugar; however, it contains a decent amount of minerals, especially manganese, zinc, potassium and iron. And it has that lovely unique flavour! You can use maple syrup in any of your desserts or sweet treats. Keep in mind that if you pair it with nuts or other protein-rich ingredients such as nut milk, it will lower the GI and slow the release of sugar into the bloodstream. I like to use this one in moderation, but it goes so wonderfully well on raw banana pancakes!

Medicine flowers is a brand of 100 per cent pure plant extracts with no preservatives, alcohol, or fillers. They come in a wonderful array of flavours such as banana, vanilla, rose, orange, raspberry, lemon, mint, lime, almond, cherry, fig, hazelnut, guava, pear, passionfruit and more. They are super concentrated, so just a few drops are needed to add a wonderful flavour to any dish. They have a much purer flavour than essences.

Mesquite is actually a legume from South America that is high in protein and fibre, has great quantities of calcium, magnesium, potassium, iron and zinc, and is rich in the amino acid lysine too. It has a GI of 25. It has a wonderful caramel flavour and goes especially well with maca, cacao, and lucuma. Throw it into your smoothies, sweet treats or raw ice-cream for an extra caramel hit and superfood boost!

Raw honey is alkalising, antiviral, antibacterial and anti-fungal and contains natural vitamins, enzymes, powerful antioxidants and other important natural nutrients. Pasteurised honey does not contain any of these important nutrients due to high-heat processing – pasteurised honey is also as unhealthy as eating refined sugar!

RAW HONEY IS GREAT FOR DIGESTION;

it's also an excellent remedy for skin wounds and all types of infections. Raw honey also has a lower GI than pasteurised honey; depending on the type, the GI can range from 35 to 58. Add to your desserts, smoothies, or sweet treats in moderation. I like to use it in my savoury marinades — just a few teaspoons to impart that wonderful flavour.

Stevia comes as a liquid or powder and is super-concentrated – 100 times sweeter than sugar. It is sugar-free and has a GI of 0. A perfect 'go-to' sweetener for those suffering from diabetes or candida; it is derived from the stevia plant, so it's a naturally occurring sweetener. Just three drops of liquid stevia equals 1 teaspoon of sugar. Add into smoothies, desserts, sweets, treats and sauces.

Yacon syrup is extracted from the tuberous roots of the yacon plant (a plant native to South America), and contains about 50 per cent FOS or fructooligosaccharides, which act as a prebiotic (that is, they help create conditions in the gut that allow good bacteria to flourish). Yacon doesn't affect blood sugar levels, and it increases bone density, improves immune system function, can help with weight loss, and helps your body absorb minerals from the food you eat. Yacon syrup has a molasses-type flavour and is lovely on its own with raw pancakes, on top of raw ice-cream, or added to smoothies, desserts and sweet treats. Yacon has a GI of 1 – extremely low.

Xylitol is not technically a raw product, but it's much healthier than refined sugar. It is actually sugar alcohol, which stimulates the sweet taste receptors on the tongue. It has a GI of 12. Xylitol is sourced from corn cobs or from birch trees, although corn cobs are more widely used because they are more sustainable. Just ensure you are choosing to buy a non-GMO brand. Xylitol is an alternative to sugar worth exploring for those with candida or diabetes. It's great for preventing tooth decay because, as it doesn't ferment, it doesn't provide a source of energy for these acid-producing bacteria in your teeth. Xylitol also increases the flow of naturally alkaline saliva, which rinses teeth of acids and helps the body to re-mineralise and preserve tooth enamel.

Xylitol looks and behaves like cane sugar in cooking, so it's great to use in 'baked' raw desserts, cookies or sweet treats. Note: xylitol can cause diarrhoea in some people when consumed in large amounts.

VINEGAR

Apple cider vinegar (ACV) should replace all other vinegars in your home. Apple cider vinegar is unpasteurised and retains the 'mother', which contains strands of proteins, enzymes, and good bacteria. You will know it has the 'mother' if the bottom of the bottle is cloudy, murky and has sediment. Apple cider vinegar contains acetic acid, which is a strong anti-microbial agent, and helps with weight loss, lowers blood sugar levels, kills candida, helps clear up acne, helps increase stomach acid production, and taken before meals, helps with digestion. Dilute it in water and drink it in dosages ranging from 1–2 teaspoons (5–10 mL) to 1–2 tablespoons (20–40 mL) per day, before meals. Even though it's quite acidic, it's alkaline-forming in the body – the only vinegar that does this. It's great in raw salad dressings.

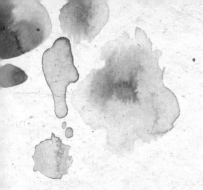

equipment glossary

There is some basic equipment you may want to invest in to turn your kitchen into an efficient raw kitchen! Go at your own pace and invest or upgrade only when you are ready. I started off with a cheap, high-powered blender and food processor. I acquired the rest as I fell in love with raw and the way it made me feel. I also used the oven method for dehydrating food for many months before investing in a dehydrator, so don't feel like you need to buy everything all at once. Here are my kitchen staples:

CHEF'S KNIFE

There are many great chef's knives out there – and expensive ones too! You don't need to spend a lot of money to get a good one, though. Look for a non-serrated knife about 15–20 cm long. Make sure the blade goes all the way into the handle. Some knives come made completely from one piece of metal; these will last a long time. A good sharpener will go a long way to keeping your knife in tip-top condition.

CHOPPING BOARD

Invest in a good solid wooden chopping board and always have it out – give it pride of place on the kitchen bench. Invest in a rubber grip you can place underneath to stop it sliding around. The wood in the chopping board also has its own beneficial antibacterial properties, so always wash gently with warm soapy water and rinse – no harsh scrubbing.

CLEAVER

Using a chef's knife to open coconuts is a sure-fire way to ruin it, so look into a good cleaver. Again, you don't need to spend a lot of money if you don't want to; just make sure it has a good solid feel to it and the blade goes all the way into the handle. Look for a 17–20 cm cleaver.

CRANK-HANDLED SPATULA

A crank-handled spatula comes in super-handy for spreading batter out on dehydrator trays to ensure a smooth, consistent finish. Great also for smoothing out cake toppings, creating a rustic finish to your cheesecakes or decorating desserts in general. Also great for scoring crackers halfway through drying time from the dehydrator.

DEHYDRATOR

This is a raw foodie's oven! Owning a dehydrator allows you to create wonderful 'cooked' dishes such as quiche, bread, crackers, chips, marinated vegetables, granola, cereals, fruit roll-ups, nut and seed mixes, cheeses and more. Being able to dehydrate at low temperatures (on or below 44°C) allows the food to remain technically raw, with all the beneficial enzymes, vitamins and minerals intact.

FOOD PROCESSOR

A food processor is going to give more of a crumbly or chunky finish to your recipes, so use it if you don't want your recipe to turn completely liquid. A good, high-powered food processor will last you for years and give you great results, so it's well worth the investment.

HIGH-POWERED BLENDER

There are some cheap, high-powered blenders in the marketplace that are great for starting out with, and then when you are ready and have saved up for it, you can invest in a really high-quality one. I like the Vitamix or the Blendtec: these are super-powerful, will last forever, and provide you with the smoothest smoothies. They can pulverise the toughest nuts, and even powder cacao beans and grind flaxseeds.

JUICER

There are two main types of juicers out there – the centrifugal juicer, which uses speed and blades to extract the juice, and the cold-press masticating juicer, which is slower and crushes your vegetables and fruits. The centrifugal juicer is great for people in a hurry, but the juice must be consumed as soon as possible as it does oxidise quite quickly. The cold-pressed juice retains its enzymes, vitamins and minerals and does not oxidise as quickly; in fact you can have your juice forty-eight hours later and it will still taste the same.

MANDOLIN

A mandolin makes life in the kitchen easy for you. It creates quick, professional-looking sliced or julienned vegetables. I like to use the Börner mandolin as it comes with three different slicing inserts for different effects and is large enough to cope with larger vegetables such as shredding cabbage for sauerkraut etc. The blades are super-sharp so always use the safety hand guard cover that comes with it.

MASON JARS

These come in super-handy for storing freshly made nut milk, coconut yoghurt, sauerkraut, blended Irish moss, salads to take to work, salad dressings, and crackers or cereal. Best of all, they are not made of plastic!

MICROPLANE GRATER

These will make zesting citrus fruit a breeze. Same for getting garlic, turmeric and ginger into your recipes without the hassle of chopping. Add a nice finishing touch to your salads by microplane-grating brazil or macadamia nuts to create a parmesan-like topping.

NUT MILK BAG

An essential for any raw kitchen, this versatile bag is made of breathable fabric, with a drawstring top. A nut milk bag allows you to separate the liquid from the pulp when making nut milks. It's also great for sprouting seeds with, as well as doubling as a cheesecloth when fermenting nut cheeses. Easy to clean – just wash with soapy water, rinse with hot water and hang on a hook to dry. A good-quality nut milk bag will last you a long time.

PARAFLEXX SHEETS

These versatile non-stick teflex sheets are very useful to lay down on your dehydrator trays when working with wet mixes. They are easy to clean with warm soapy water; simply dry them and they can then be re-used. You can use baking paper instead but it's not very economical in the long run.

PARING KNIFE

A general-purpose knife, great for small, detailed work such as peeling and coring. I'm particularly fond of using the paring knife to split open vanilla beans and scrape out the paste. A paring knife usually comes in sizes between 7–12 centimetres.

RUBBER SPATULA

This will help you get everything out of your blender, food processor or mixing bowl. Nothing gets wasted this way.

VEGIE SPIRALISER

This neat piece of equipment turns your vegetables into noodles or spaghetti. A great way to get the kids into eating healthy spaghetti. Carrots, zucchini, sweet potato, beetroot, daikon, parsnip and cucumber work particularly well this way.

techniques

Let's look at the raw food techniques we use to help ease the digestive load on the body, unlock and even enhance the nutritional content of a food, as well as give raw food a cooked texture and taste.

ALMONDS: 8–12 hours

BRAZIL NUTS: 2 hours

CASHEW NUTS: 2 hours

CHIA: 10 minutes–8 hours

HAZELNUTS: 2–4 hours

MACADAMIA NUTS: 2 hours

PECANS: 2–4 hours

PUMPKIN SEEDS: 4–6 hours

SUNFLOWER SEEDS: 4–6 hours

WALNUTS: 4–10 hours

SOAKING

We soak all nuts and seeds, even grain-like seeds such as quinoa, amaranth, millet and buckwheat, as most plants have enzyme inhibitors, which are primarily there to protect themselves in the plant world. However, these inhibitors can block mineral absorption in our bodies as well as making digestion harder than it needs to be. By soaking them we are unlocking all the wonderful benefits of the nuts and seeds, and easing the digestive load on the body. And they taste good this way, too. Soaking seeds is also the primary step in creating health-giving sprouts.

Once soaked, drain and store in an airtight container in the fridge; they will last about a week this way. Eat as is or make into nut milk, dressings or desserts. Or if you have a dehydrator, after soaking and draining, line a dehydrator tray and dehydrate your nuts for 24 hours at 105°F. Here is a rough guide for soaking times for nuts and seeds:

Soaking dried fruits and dried vegetables for a few hours beforehand also makes working with them much easier when creating recipes that require a sweeter, juicier finish.

SPROUTING

Making sprouts at home is one of the easiest and cheapest ways to get a big nutritional bang for your buck! All you need is a sprouting jar or mason jar, a screw-top lid with holes in it, a packet of seeds (such as alfalfa, fenugreek, pea or mustard) and some good-quality filtered water. Simply pop the seeds in the jar, fill the jar with water, soak overnight in the jar and then drain and rinse twice a day until they have sprouted! You will know this is happening with the tails start to form, usually around about two to three days. Consuming sprouts means you are eating food at its freshest, highest life force peak, teeming with enzymes, vitamins and minerals, making them super easy to eat and digest. Throw into crackers, salads or smoothies.

DEHYDRATING

Using a dehydrator gives raw food a cooked taste, texture and crunch, but because it's done at low temperatures (around or below 48°C/118°F – 44°C/111°F), the food is still technically raw.

Dehydrating is also a way to preserve food, so once dehydrated it will generally have a long and stable shelf life, if kept in an airtight container.

At the time of writing I use and recommend the Excalibur 9 Tray Dehydrator with timer. It's reliable and easy to use, and has a consistent drying time. The beauty of the design is that it has flat square trays that allow you to bulk-dry crackers, cereals, breads, cheeses, fruit roll-ups and kale chips, all in one hit.

Owning a dehydrator is really like having a raw foodie's oven and it opens up a whole new world of creating and making raw recipes. Best of all, most of them fit in your microwave space (and a dehydrator is a much healthier option than a microwave).

If you want to get started with dehydrated food recipes but don't have a dehydrator, you can use the oven method, with the door slightly open and at the lowest setting – usually at about 50°C or lower. However, oven temperatures vary a lot and can be inconsistent, so keep an eye on it and check every hour; the food won't technically be raw but it's a much gentler way of creating your dishes than blasting them at 180°C+.

OPENING A COCONUT

It's very common to see young Thai coconuts available everywhere these days. However, opening them still remains a mystery to many. Opening a coconut requires a good-quality cleaver and a few simple knife techniques. The first step is to tip the coconut on its side on a chopping board and shave down the triangle or cone part until the brown nut is exposed. Then tip the coconut upright again and place one hand at the base. With the cleaver in the other hand, ensure it's at a 45° angle and aim the heel of the cleaver into the top part of the nut, about three-quarters of the way down.

Bring the cleaver down at this angle to create a crack. Continue around the coconut on the same plane at the same angle until a natural hairline crack or opening forms. Once this happens, you should be able to wedge the cleaver into the crack and use a rocking motion forward and back to pop open the newly formed lid. Pour the coconut water into a jug, then scoop the flesh out with an ice-cream scoop.

Nothing beats fresh coconuts: they are raw, live, and teeming with enzymes, electrolytes, potassium, vitamins, minerals and good fats. They are antiviral and anti-fungal, as well as reducing inflammation and helping the body burn fat.

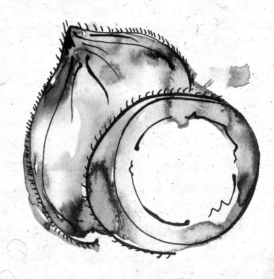

menu plan

MONDAY

breakfast
Go green smoothie
p. 48

. . . .

snack
Carrot muffin with
orange cashew cream
p. 190 (made the week
before)

. . . .

lunch
San choy bow p. 96

. . . .

dinner
Curried vegetable
patties with slaw and
minty coconut yoghurt
p. 138 (make extra for
lunch tomorrow
if needed)

. . . .

after dinner tip
Prepare ingredients
for tomorrow's chia
brekky p. 72

TUESDAY

breakfast
Lime coconut dream
chia porridgep. 72

. . . .

snack
Morning sunshine tea
p. 56

. . . .

lunch
Curried vegetable
patties with slaw and
minty coconut
yoghurt leftovers
p. 138

. . . .

snack
Kale and coconut
chips p. 160 (made the
week before)

. . . .

dinner
Zucchini pasta
with broad beans,
asparagus and peas
in a light cashew
cream sauce p. 106
(make extra for lunch
tomorrow if needed)
Sleepy tea p. 56

. . . .

after dinner tip
Prepare ingredients
for Thursday's tropical
rawsli brekky
p. 02 and p. 204

WEDNESDAY

breakfast
Aloha yoga smoothie
p. 51

. . . .

lunch
Zucchini pasta
with broad beans,
asparagus and peas in
a light cashew cream
sauce leftovers p. 106

. . . .

snack
Kale and coconut
chips p. 160 (made the
week before)

. . . .

dinner
Spicy goji, carrot,
rocket and fennel salad
p. 92 (make extra for
lunch tomorrow if
needed)

. . . .

after dinner tip
Prepare ingredients
for tomorrow's corn
burrito lunch
p. 216

THURSDAY

breakfast
Tropical rawsli with
almond milk
p. 62 and p. 204

....

lunch
Corn burrito wraps
with Spicy goji, carrot,
rocket and fennel salad
leftovers
p. 216 and p. 92

....

dinner
Vietnamese rice paper
rolls with almond
dipping sauce p. 90
(make extra for lunch
tomorrow if needed)

....

dessert
Choc-orange bliss
balls p. 168 (made the
week before)
Sleepy tea p. 56

FRIDAY

breakfast
Liver lover juice p. 50

....

snack
Carrot muffin with
orange cashew cream
p. 190 (made the
week before)

....

lunch
Vietnamese rice paper
rolls with almond
dipping sauce
leftovers p. 90

....

dinner
FREE MEAL
follow the 80/20 rule

SATURDAY

breakfast
Tropical rawsli with
almond milk
p. 62 and p. 204

....

lunch
Vege medley quiche
p. 94 (save leftovers
for tomorrow)

....

dinner
FREE MEAL
follow the 80/20 rule

....

after dinner tip
Prepare ingredients
for tomorrow's Sunday
morning easy brunch
p. 64

SUNDAY

breakfast
Sunday morning easy
p. 64

....

lunch
Vege medley quiche
leftovers p. 94

....

after lunch tips
• Bulk batch soak and
dehydrate nuts and
seeds for next week.
Sprout a batch of
buckwheat for
next week.

• Make a nice salad
dressing or sauce
for next week, choose
from our yummy
selection on
pp. 221–226

• Make a sweet treat
for next week, so
you have something
naughty-but-nice on
hand. Try the ginger
goji maca cookies,
p. 164

....

dinner
Vegetable moussaka
p. 140
Sleepy tea p. 56

chapter

juice
smoo
& dri

rosella kombucha smoothie

This refreshing, rejuvenating smoothie is great as a post-workout drink.
It has the added bonus of kombucha, which is teeming with good bacteria
for gut health and happiness.

SERVES 2

flesh and water of 1 young coconut

1 medjool date, pitted

4 handfuls of blueberries

8 drops of medicine flowers
vanilla extract (or 1 teaspoon
vanilla essence)

12 drops of medicine flowers
coconut extract (optional)

1 teaspoon bee pollen

1 tablespoon acai or maqui powder

1 tablespoon hemp protein powder

1 cup (250 ml) rosella kombucha
(see page 54)

5 ice cubes

Place the fruit in a high-powered blender, then add the extracts,
pollen and powders and blend until smooth. Add the kombucha and
ice cubes and blend to mix through. Adjust to taste, then pour into
glasses and serve.

Note

For a sugar-free or low-sugar option, omit the dates and blueberries and
replace with 3–6 drops of stevia liquid and half an avocado. If you have
medicine flowers extracts, add 8–12 drops of blueberry extract.

go green smoothie

This is a great meal substitute and a really good way to get you alkaline. The quantity of water depends on your preferred consistency – less water will be more like a smoothie, but if you'd like it to be more like a juice, add more water

SERVES 8

1 zucchini (courgette), roughly chopped

1–2 kale leaves

large handful of mint leaves

1 teaspoon maca powder

1 teaspoon camu camu powder

1 teaspoon spirulina powder

2 teaspoons chia seeds

½ avocado, peeled

½ frozen banana

1 green apple, roughly chopped

1 green pear, roughly chopped

1 lime, peeled

6 medjool dates, pitted

knob of ginger, thinly sliced

1 heaped teaspoon cold-pressed coconut oil

pinch of Himalayan crystal salt

a few squirts of stevia liquid

3–4 cups (750 ml–1 litre) filtered water

a few ice cubes (optional)

Place all the ingredients in a high-powered blender and blend, baby, blend! Pour into glasses and drink immediately.

Note

For a very low-sugar or sugar-free option, omit the frozen banana, dates and pear. If you have medicine flowers extracts, add 8–12 drops of banana extract.

liver lover juice

Beetroot contains an ingredient called betaine, which helps the liver to restore its normal function, and aids in the detoxification process and processing fats. Coriander and chlorella help draw toxins out of the body. Beetroot and spinach are also great blood builders so, combined with the vitamin C from the lemon, this is a great drink to have every day if you suffer from low iron levels.

SERVES 2

1 large carrot
1 beetroot, peeled
1 green apple
1 cucumber
handful of baby spinach
1 lemon, peeled
handful of mint leaves
handful of coriander leaves
knob of ginger, thinly sliced
1 teaspoon chlorella powder
a few squirts of stevia liquid (optional)

Run the vegetables, lemon, herbs and ginger through a cold-press masticating juicer. Whisk in the chlorella and sweeten with a little stevia, if you like. Pour into glasses and drink immediately.

green cleanser juice

Loaded with greens and herbs to help you detoxify chemicals and heavy metals, this juice is extremely cleansing and refreshing. It is also low GI, high in minerals, and great for your skin and joints, and any inflammation.

SERVES 4

½ bunch celery
2 cucumbers
4–6 kale leaves
1 bunch mint
½ bunch coriander
½ bunch dill
1 lemon, peeled
4 oranges, peeled
1 cm piece of turmeric root

Run all the ingredients through a cold-press masticating juicer. Pour into glasses and serve straight away.

Note

For a sugar-free or very low-sugar option, omit the oranges and replace with 1 extra lemon and 3 limes, or add a few drops of 100% pure organic essential oil of lime.

summer sensation

Nothing says summer to me more than watermelon and strawberries! This refreshing concoction is also a nice base to combine with rosella kombucha to make a wonderful probiotic-rich drink. Just add ¼ cup (60 ml) of rosella kombucha (see page 54) at the end of blending and serve. *Pictured page iv.*

SERVES 2

650 g watermelon flesh
250 g strawberries, hulled
3 cm piece of ginger, peeled
2½–3 tablespoons mint leaves, plus extra sprigs to garnish
ice cubes, to serve

Place the fruit, ginger and mint in a high-powered blender and blend until smooth. Pour into ice-filled glasses and serve garnished with extra mint sprigs.

aloha yoga

This is a great recovery smoothie for after yoga or a workout. Coconut water is super-hydrating and helps balance electrolytes. Flaxseeds are high in omega 3, fibre and help the body burn fat. Lucuma powder is a delicious creamy citrus superfood and low-GI sweetener, and the goji berries will help nourish your adrenals. *Pictured page 8.*

SERVES 2

flesh of 1 young coconut
1¾ cups (435 ml) coconut water
2 frozen bananas, skins removed
1 tablespoon flaxseed meal
2 teaspoons lucuma powder
handful of goji berries
1 teaspoon vanilla extract
1 teaspoon coconut extract (optional)

Place all the ingredients in a high-powered blender or food processor and blend until smooth. Serve immediately.

Note

For a low-sugar option, omit the bananas and replace with half an avocado. If you still want the banana flavour without the high sugar add 8–12 drops of medicine flowers banana extract.

turmeric tonic

Turmeric has anti-inflammatory, anti-cancer, antibacterial and antiviral properties. It is also immune boosting and detoxifying, and should be added to your daily diet in any way possible. This lovely spiced tonic is a great way to start: you can serve it warm or chilled, perhaps with a dusting of cinnamon and a cinnamon stick.

SERVES 2

1 cup (250 ml) almond milk (see page 204)

1 cup (250 ml) filtered water (warm or chilled, depending on your preference)

2 thin slices turmeric root

¼ teaspoon ground turmeric

¼ teaspoon thinly sliced ginger (or ¼ teaspoon dried ginger)

2 medjool dates, pitted

2 tablespoons raw honey

½ teaspoon yacon syrup or other low-GI sweetener of your choice

¼ teaspoon ground cinnamon

¼ teaspoon ground cardamom

generous pinch of ground star anise

pinch of Himalayan crystal salt

pinch of ground black pepper

pinch of ground cloves

Place all the ingredients in a high-powered blender and blend until smooth. Serve warm or chilled.

Note

For a low-sugar or sugar-free option, omit the dates and honey and add 3 drops of stevia liquid.

rosella kombucha

Kombucha is a very medicinal drink and contains many beneficial yeasts and good bacteria – just 100 ml of kombucha provides approximately 4 trillion good bacteria! In addition, it contains no caffeine and can benefit those with candida or gut issues. Always take it like a tonic and not a drink. It's quite powerful so start off with a small amount (1½ tablespoons a day) and work your way up to as much as you like or can tolerate.

SERVES 4

¼ cup (55 g) raw organic sugar

2 tea bags (black or green tea)

1 tablespoon dried rosella tea leaves or 1 fruit tea tea bag

1 litre non-chlorinated water

kombucha mother or SCOBY (see note)

½ cup (125 ml) kombucha (purchased or from previous batch)

Place the sugar and tea bags and/or leaves in a large glass jug. Boil the water and pour into the jug. Stir using a wooden or non-reactive metal spoon, then leave to steep until it is tepid (test by dipping a clean finger into the liquid). Pour into a clean brewing jar. Add the kombucha mother or SCOBY and the kombucha from the previous batch and gently stir again. Cover with muslin cloth or any breathable material and store in a cupboard away from smells and other ferments and allow to ferment for 7–10 days. The longer you leave it the less sweet it will taste.

When it reaches your desired flavour, strain the kombucha through a fine mesh cloth into a flip-top glass bottle or screw-top jars, pop in the fridge and it's ready to drink. Make sure you leave the mother behind in the original brewing jar with ½ cup (125 ml) of the original kombucha liquid so you can start another batch, as above.

Note

SCOBY stands for Symbiotic Colony of Bacteria and Yeast. You'll need a SCOBY (it looks like a gelatinous brown lump) to create your kombucha as the SCOBY eats the tea and sugar to create the kombucha flavour. A healthy SCOBY will produce a baby SCOBY after 7 days of fermentation in the tea and sugar mixture. Play around with the flavours after fermentation – for instance, try adding more fruit, citrus peel or ginger. To get started you can buy a fresh SCOBY online or use a friend's homemade one.

herbal teas:

morning sunshine

This is a wonderful way to start the day but I must warn you that this tea contains caffeine, so if you are sensitive to caffeine, replace the green and Yerba mate teas with dandelion tea.

SERVES 2

1 tablespoon green tea leaves

1 tablespoon Yerba mate tea leaves (optional)

1 tablespoon dried peppermint

2 teaspoons fennel seeds

2 cups (500 ml) water, boiled and cooled slightly

lemon slices and raw honey, to serve (optional)

Combine the green tea leaves, peppermint and fennel seeds to make a blend. Place 1 teaspoon of tea blend in each cup and pour over the hot water. Allow to steep for 5 minutes, then strain and serve with lemon slices and honey to taste, if desired.

immune boost

Ginger is a digestive warming aromatic and echinacea helps give the immune system a boost, warding off cold and flu.

SERVES 2

1 tablespoon lemongrass and ginger tea leaves (alternatively, use 2 teaspoons dried ginger root or fresh ginger and 2 teaspoons dried or fresh lemongrass)

1 tablespoon echinacea

pinch of cayenne pepper

4 slices fresh turmeric, roughly chopped

2 cups (500 ml) water, boiled and cooled slightly

raw honey, to serve (optional)

Combine the tea leaves, echinacea, cayenne pepper and turmeric to make a blend. Place 1 teaspoon of tea blend in each cup and pour over the hot water. Allow to steep for 5 minutes, or longer if preferred, then strain and serve with honey to taste, if desired.

sleepy tea

As the name suggests, this is a nice tea to relax with at the end of a long day. I often have a cup just before bed time.

SERVES 2

1 tablespoon dried camomile flowers or tea leaves

1 tablespoon dried hops

1 teaspoon dried peppermint

4 slices of orange peel

2 teaspoons catnip (optional)

2 cups (500 ml) water, boiled and cooled slightly

raw honey, to serve (optional)

Combine the camomile, hops, peppermint, orange peel and catnip (if using) to make a blend. Place 1 teaspoon of tea blend in each cup and pour over the hot water. Allow to steep for 5 minutes, or longer if preferred, then serve with honey to taste, if desired.

choc heaven smoothie

I love this because it tastes very naughty but is actually very low in sugar (really, the only sugar comes from the garnishes). Plus it has tons of superfood power in there: high antioxidants of the cacao, hormone-balancing maca, adaptogenic herbs (think stress relief!) and immune-boosting reishi mushroom from the Ancient Wisdom superfood blend, minerals and fibre from the chia, and good fats from the avocado.

SERVES 2

2 cups (500 ml) almond milk
(see page 204)

½ avocado, peeled

2 tablespoons cacao powder

1 tablespoon chia seeds

1 tablespoon maca powder

2 teaspoons Ancient Wisdom
superfood (or 2 teaspoons powdered
medicinal mushrooms)

8–12 drops of medicine flowers
vanilla extract (or 1 teaspoon
vanilla essence)

6 squirts of stevia liquid, or to taste

shredded coconut, goji berries and
cacao nibs, to garnish

Place all the ingredients (except the garnishes) in a high-powered blender and blend until smooth. Pour into two glasses and top with the garnishes. Serve immediately.

brea

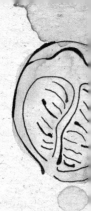

chapter

N°2

kfast

tropical rawsli

This wheat-free, dairy-free, refined-sugar-free muesli is loaded with good fats. A great source of digestive enzymes, selenium, magnesium and B vitamins, it's totally nutritious!

SERVES 4

¾ cup (105 g) chopped medjool dates, soaked for 20 minutes in hot filtered water, drained

1 cup (140 g) macadamias, soaked for 2 hours in filtered water, drained and roughly chopped

1 cup (150 g) sunflower seeds, soaked for 4 hours in filtered water, then rinsed and drained

1 pineapple, peeled and roughly chopped

1 cup (75 g) shredded coconut

1 teaspoon vanilla bean powder

1 teaspoon coconut extract

1 teaspoon mixed spice

1 teaspoon ground cinnamon

juice of ¼ lemon

½ cup (175 g) raw honey, plus extra if needed

1 teaspoon Himalayan crystal salt

Combine all the ingredients in a bowl. Add a little more honey if it needs more 'stick'.

Spread out the muesli on a dehydrator tray lined with baking paper or paraflexx sheets. Dehydrate at 54°C (130°F) for 1 hour, then reduce the temperature to 43°C (110°F) and dehydrate for 24 hours or until dried.

If you don't have a dehydrator you could serve the rawsli just as it is with any of the nut milks (see page 204) and a dollop of coconut yoghurt (see page 212).

sunday morning easy

This is just the thing for a relaxed Sunday brunch with friends or anyone who loves a savoury breakfast.

SERVES 4

pesto (see page 216),
ricotta (see page 206) and
rocket (optional), to serve

MARINATED MUSHROOMS

2 tablespoons tamari

2 tablespoons lemon juice

1 tablespoon mixed dried herbs

1 teaspoon raw honey

2 tablespoons olive oil

4 swiss brown or portobello
mushrooms, stems removed

HERBED SEMI-DRIED TOMATOES

2 tablespoons apple cider vinegar

2 tablespoons olive oil, plus extra
to serve

1 tablespoon basil, very thinly sliced

1 teaspoon raw honey

pinch of Himalayan crystal salt,
plus extra to serve

4 roma (plum) tomatoes, quartered

To prepare the mushrooms, combine the tamari, lemon juice, herbs, honey and olive oil in a bowl. Brush the marinade over the mushrooms, then placed on a dehydrator tray lined with baking paper or paraflexx sheets and dehydrate at 43°C (110°F) for 2–4 hours. Set aside.

To prepare the tomatoes, combine the vinegar, olive oil, basil, honey and salt in a bowl. Brush the marinade over the tomatoes, then place on a lined dehydrator tray and dehydrate at 43°C (110°F) for 2–4 hours. Set aside.

When you're ready to eat, place a mushroom on each plate with the underside facing up, then spread with the pesto and then the ricotta. Top with the semi-dried tomatoes and, if you like, serve with rocket leaves, a little salt and a splash of olive oil.

fig jam sprouted buckwheat bowl

This nut-free cereal is made with buckwheat, a seed-like grain that is very alkalising, high in vitamins and minerals, and particularly high in magnesium. Be sure to choose buckwheat that has not been roasted if you wish to sprout it. Sprouting enhances its vitamin and mineral content further and makes it super-easy to digest. Paired with figs and spices, this great gluten-free breakfast is a lovely way to start your day.

SERVES 4

1½ cups (300 g) dried organic figs, soaked overnight in filtered water

2 cm piece of ginger, peeled and roughly chopped

5 cups (500 g) sprouted buckwheat (see page 40)

juice of ½ lemon

1 teaspoon ground cinnamon, plus extra for dusting

1 teaspoon mixed spice

½ teaspoon ground star anise

pinch of Himalayan crystal salt

2 tablespoons raw coconut nectar, plus extra to serve (optional)

almond milk (see page 204), to serve

2 fresh figs, halved

Drain the dried figs and thinly slice them, reserving the soaking liquid. Place ⅔ cup (160 ml) of the soaking liquid in a small high-powered blender with most of the sliced fig (reserve ¼ cup (50 g) for later). Add the ginger and blend to a paste.

Transfer the paste and reserved figs to a large bowl and stir in the sprouted buckwheat, lemon juice, spices, salt and coconut nectar. Adjust to taste.

Line two dehydrator trays with baking paper or paraflexx sheets. Pour half the mixture on each tray and smooth out to the edges – it should be about 1–2 mm thick.

Dehydrate at 40°C (105°F) for 10–14 hours or until dry and crisp. Remove from the sheets and break up into chunks. Store in an airtight container in the pantry for up to 3 months.

Serve with almond milk, fresh figs and a dusting of extra cinnamon. Drizzle with a little extra coconut nectar, if desired.

Note

To make this super-low GI, low sugar and gluten free, replace the fig paste with 8–10 drops of medicine flowers fig extract or more to your taste, and stir in 3 drops of stevia liquid, ¼ cup (60 ml) yacon syrup and ½ cup (100 g) Irish moss paste (see page 26).

grawnola

Another raw take on one of my favourite breakfast cererals: granola. Except this is much more nutritionally dense and gluten free!

SERVES 6

1 cup (160 g) almonds, soaked for 8–12 hours in filtered water, then drained and rinsed

½ cup (70 g) pumpkin seeds, soaked for 4–6 hours in filtered water, then drained and rinsed

½ cup (75 g) sunflower seeds, soaked for 4 hours in filtered water, then drained and rinsed

½ cup (60 g) pecans, soaked for 2–4 hours in filtered water, then drained and rinsed

½ cup (70 g) pitted medjool dates, soaked for 20 minutes in hot filtered water, drained

¼ cup (25 g) goji berries, soaked for 20 minutes in hot filtered water, drained

¼ cup (35 g) dried cranberries, soaked for 20 minutes in hot filtered water, drained

1 cup (75 g) shredded coconut

2 teaspoons ground cinnamon

1 teaspoon mixed spice

¼ cup (60 ml) raw coconut nectar

1 tablespoon coconut oil, melted

1 tablespoon lemon juice

1 apple, cored and roughly chopped

1 pear, cored and roughly chopped

thinly sliced apple, to garnish (optional)

Place all the nuts and seeds in a food processor and blitz until combined but still a bit chunky. Transfer to a bowl. Place the remaining ingredients (except the garnish) in the food processor and blitz until combined. Add to the nuts and seeds and stir to combine.

You can eat the grawnola as is (and store in an airtight container in the fridge for 4–5 days). Alternatively, spread out the grawnola on a dehydrator tray lined with baking paper or paraflexx sheets and dehydrate at 43°C (110°F) for 24 hours or until dry. Flip the trays halfway through the drying time to remove the paraflexx sheets or baking paper.

Served garnished with sliced apple, if liked.

Note

To make a low-sugar version of this recipe, omit the dates and cranberries, and add 1 tablespoon ground cinnamon, 3 drops of stevia liquid and 8–12 drops of medicine flowers apple extract.

coconut crepes with cashew cream and maqui blueberries

This is absolutely delicious, a total treat, and something that I save for a special occasion. I suggest berries here, but really you can use whatever fruit you like.

SERVES 4

flesh of 2 young coconuts
(reserve the coconut water)

1 tablespoon yacon syrup
or raw coconut nectar

pinch of Himalayan crystal salt

½ banana

1 cup (150 g) blueberries

mint sprigs, to serve (optional)

BLUEBERRY SAUCE

1 cup (150 g) blueberries

2 teaspoons maqui powder

juice of ½ lime

⅓ cup (80 ml) filtered water

pinch of Himalayan crystal salt

CASHEW CREAM

1 cup (150 g) cashews, soaked
for 2 hours in filtered water,
then rinsed and drained

⅓ cup (70 g) coconut oil, melted

1 teaspoon vanilla extract

finely grated zest and juice of 1 lime

pinch of Himalayan crystal salt

3 drops of stevia liquid

2 tablespoons maple syrup

½ cup (125 ml) filtered water
(optional)

Combine the coconut flesh, syrup or nectar, salt and banana in a high-powered blender, gradually adding the coconut water. Blend until smooth – you want the mixture to be the consistency of thick cream; it shouldn't be too thin. Line dehydrator trays with baking paper or paraflexx sheets. Using an 10 cm ring mould, pour the batter into the mould to a thickness of 2–3 mm to create about 16 small crepes. (Alternatively draw circles on the paper and spread the mixture within the guide.) Dehydrate at 43°C (110°F) until the tops are dry, checking every few hours, then flip them over and continue until both sides are dehydrated but the crepes are still pliable. All up, this should take 9–12 hours. The crepes will keep for at least 3 months in an airtight container in the fridge.

Place the berries in a bowl and warm in a dehydrator at 43°C (110°F) for 20 minutes.

To make the blueberry sauce, blend all the ingredients until smooth.

For the cashew cream, place all the ingredients except the water in a high-powered blender and blend, gradually adding enough water to make a thick cream (if needed). Store in the fridge if not eating straight away.

When you're ready to serve, place a crepe on each plate. Spread cashew cream in the middle, top with some berries and a sprig of mint (if using), then roll up the crepes, wetting the edge to seal. Serve with the blueberry sauce.

lime coconut dream chia porridge

I love the versatility of chia seeds: they are great for thickening sauces, smoothies and desserts, or simply sprinkling over salads. Soaked for 20 minutes or overnight in water or other yummy liquid ingredients, they make a great base for a healthy porridge.

SERVES 4

flesh of 2 young coconuts

2½ cups (625 ml) coconut water, plus extra if needed

¼ cup (60 ml) lime juice

12 drops of lime essential oil (optional)

½ cup (60 g) chia seeds

1 cup (150 g) cashews, roughly chopped

½ cup (50 g) goji berries, plus extra to serve

1 teaspoon vanilla extract or 8–12 medicine flowers vanilla extract

pinch of Himalayan crystal salt

¼ cup (60 ml) raw coconut nectar, plus extra to serve

finely grated zest of 1 lime

1–2 teaspoons ground cinnamon, plus extra to serve

1 banana, diced, plus extra sliced banana to serve

nut milk (see page 204), shredded coconut and lime wedges, to serve

Blend the coconut flesh, coconut water, lime juice and lime oil (if using) until smooth. Add a little extra coconut water if the mixture is too thick. Whisk in the chia seeds, then stir in the chopped cashews, goji berries, vanilla, salt, coconut nectar, lime zest and cinnamon. Place in the fridge overnight to set.

Just before serving, stir in the diced banana. Spoon into serving bowls and pour nut milk around the porridge. Top with sliced banana, shredded coconut, goji berries, a dusting of cinnamon and a swirl of coconut nectar. Serve with lime wedges.

crumbly crunch topping

This easy crumble topping can be enjoyed at any time of the day. It's great sprinkled over breakfast cereals, but also adds a fantastic crunch to desserts such as macadamia ice-cream, mango parfait, apple cinnamon superfood cake or key lime slice (see pages 182, 194, 172 and 186). A dollop of Irish moss cream or coconut yoghurt rounds it out perfectly.

SERVES 8

2½ cups (300 g) pecans (or other nut of your choice), soaked for 2–4 hours in filtered water, then rinsed and drained

½ cup (70 g) coconut sugar

2 teaspoons ground cinnamon

¼ teaspoon ground nutmeg

1 teaspoon mixed spice

¼ teaspoon Himalayan crystal salt

2 tablespoons coconut oil, melted

Spread out the nuts on a dehydrator tray lined with baking paper or paraflexx sheets. Dehydrate at 40°C (105°F) for 6 hours.

Place all the ingredients except the coconut oil in a food processor and process until the mixture resemble large breadcrumbs. Add the coconut oil and pulse to combine. Adjust to taste, then store in an airtight container, where it will keep for months.

Note

To make a sugar-free version, omit the coconut sugar and replace with ½ cup (100 g) powdered xylitol.

brekky burrito

This is just the thing for a filling and nutritious weekend breakfast: a homemade corn burrito wrap enclosing corn scramble, tomato and avocado salad and spinach. It also makes a great lunch dish. The chilli adds a wake-up bite, but you can leave it out if you're not a fan of heat!

SERVES 4

3 roma (plum) tomatoes, finely diced

1 avocado, peeled, stone removed, finely diced

1–2 tablespoons lime juice

1 teaspoon ground cumin

handful of coriander leaves, roughly chopped, plus extra leaves to garnish

1 teaspoon raw coconut nectar

¼ red onion, diced

1 small red chilli, seeded and finely chopped (optional)

12 corn burrito wraps (see page 216)

baby spinach leaves, to serve

extra virgin olive oil, to garnish (optional)

CORN SCRAMBLE

1 cup (150 g) cashews, soaked for 2 hours in filtered water, then rinsed and drained

1 cup (200 g) corn kernels (from 1–1½ corn cobs)

½ white onion, roughly chopped

1 clove garlic, crushed

2 tablespoons nutritional yeast

1 tablespoon onion powder

1 teaspoon tamari

1 teaspoon apple cider vinegar

1 teaspoon raw honey

small handful of basil leaves, roughly chopped

1 small red chilli, seeded and finely chopped (optional)

pinch of ground turmeric

pinch of Himalayan crystal salt and ground black pepper (optional)

To make the corn scramble, place the cashews, corn and onion in a food processor and process until they resemble large breadcrumbs. Transfer to a bowl, then add the remaining ingredients and stir to combine. Adjust the seasoning if required.

Place the tomato, avocado, lime juice, cumin, coriander, coconut nectar, onion and chilli (if using) in a bowl and stir gently to combine.

To serve, fill the wraps with spinach leaves, corn scramble and tomato salad. Garnish with coriander and serve immediately with a splash of olive oil, if liked.

coconut yoghurt, berry smash and buckini mix parfait

This breakfast dish looks really pretty layered in glass mason jars. It's a great one to take to work and eat on the run: just layer it up in the jar and place in the fridge the night before, seal with the screw-top lid and away you go!

SERVES 4

2 cups (560 g) coconut yoghurt (see page 212)

1 cup (130 g) strawberries

1 cup (135 g) raspberries and/or blueberries

coconut nectar, to serve (optional)

ground cinnamon or crumbly crunch topping (see page 74), to garnish (optional)

BUCKINI MIX

¾ cup (75 g) sprouted buckwheat (see page 40)

⅓ cup (55 g) almonds, soaked for 8–12 hours in filtered water, then rinsed, drained and roughly chopped

2 tablespoons sunflower seeds, soaked for 4 hours in filtered water, then rinsed, drained and roughly chopped

1 tablespoon pumpkin seeds, soaked for 4–6 hours in filtered water, then rinsed, drained and roughly chopped

2 tablespoons shredded coconut

1 tablespoon chia seeds

1 teaspoon ground cinnamon

pinch of Himalayan crystal salt

1 tablespoon coconut oil, melted

To make the buckini mix, spread out the buckwheat, almonds, sunflower seeds and pumpkin seeds on a dehydrator tray lined with baking paper or paraflexx sheets. Dehydrate at 43°C (110°F) for 12–20 hours. Combine with the remaining ingredients in a bowl or glass jar.

Layer the buckini mix, yoghurt and berries in four glasses or bowls. Serve straight away or store in the fridge overnight. Drizzle with coconut nectar and finish with a dusting of cinnamon or crumbly crunch topping, if liked.

cashew flatbread with antipasti spread

This lovely dish makes a great savoury breakfast alternative to all the sweeter cereals, but may also be enjoyed for lunch. If you don't have time to make the flatbread, the antipasto dishes could also be served with crunchy seed crackers (see page 158). Keep the leftover ingredients separate in the fridge and use them for cracker or salad toppings.

SERVES 4

cashew flatbreads (see page 217), to serve

MARINATED MUSHROOMS
1 tablespoon olive oil
1 tablespoon lemon juice
1 clove garlic, crushed
½ teaspoon dried oregano
125 g button mushrooms, sliced
small handful of flat-leaf parsley leaves, finely chopped
pinch of Himalayan crystal salt

OLIVE TAPENADE
1 cup (120 g) pitted black olives
1 clove garlic, crushed
1 tablespoon lemon juice
1 tablespoon olive oil
1 tablespoon finely chopped flat-leaf parsley
Himalayan crystal salt and ground black pepper

CHERRY TOMATO SALAD
150 g cherry tomatoes, halved
½ red capsicum (pepper), seeds and vein removed, finely diced
¼ red onion, finely diced
dash of apple cider vinegar
dash of olive oil
handful of basil leaves, torn
pinch of Himalayan crystal salt

To prepare the mushrooms, place the olive oil, lemon juice, garlic and oregano in a bowl and mix well. Add the mushrooms and parsley and stir to combine. Set aside to marinate for at least 20 minutes and up to 2 hours.

To make the tapenade, place all the ingredients in a food processor and blend to form a paste. Adjust to taste. Place in an airtight container and store in the fridge until needed.

To prepare the cherry tomato salad, combine all the ingredients in a bowl and set aside for about 15–20 minutes.

When you're ready to eat, serve the cashew flatbread with the various toppings.

quinoa porridge with goji berries and macadamias

This beautiful, warming breakfast dish is great in winter. Quinoa is a delicious gluten-free grain, and contains heart-healthy omega 3, essential minerals such as manganese, magnesium, iron, phosphorus, potassium, calcium, zinc, copper and selenium. It's also high in antioxidants. Soaking quinoa before cooking removes the bitter taste and softens the grain.

SERVES 2-4

1 cup (190 g) quinoa, soaked for 10–20 minutes in filtered water, then drained

1 tablespoon coconut oil, melted, plus extra to serve

2 cups (500 ml) filtered water

¼ cup (35 g) macadamias, soaked for 2 hours in filtered water, then rinsed, drained and roughly chopped

1 teaspoon ground cinnamon, plus extra to garnish (optional)

1 teaspoon mixed spice

pinch of ground cardamom

¼ cup (25 g) goji berries

2–3 tablespoons raw coconut nectar

1 teaspoon vanilla extract or 6–10 drops of medicine flowers vanilla extract

pinch of Himalayan crystal salt

1 cup (250 ml) almond milk (see page 204), plus extra to serve

fresh or stewed fruit and coconut flakes, to serve (optional)

Place the quinoa, coconut oil and water in a saucepan and bring gently to a simmer. Reduce the heat to low and cook, stirring, until the quinoa has absorbed all the water. Add the macadamias, spices, goji berries, coconut nectar, vanilla and salt and stir well. Gradually add enough almond milk to reach your preferred consistency.

Spoon the porridge into warm bowls and pour extra almond milk around it. Serve with an extra tablespoon of coconut oil, your choice of fresh or stewed fruit, coconut flakes and a final dusting of ground cinnamon, if liked.

Note

For a low-sugar version, use 2–3 tablespoons yacon syrup instead of the coconut nectar, or 3–6 drops of stevia liquid, and omit the stewed fruit.

N° 3 chapter

genius gazpacho

Filling and nutritious, this is the perfect summer soup. Serve it at room temperature or gently heat your soup bowls in the dehydrator at 67°C (153°F) for 10–20 minutes.

SERVES 4-6

¼ white onion, roughly chopped

2 zucchini (courgettes), peeled and roughly chopped

2 red capsicums (peppers), seeds and veins removed, roughly chopped

2 tablespoons shiro miso paste

juice of 1 lemon

1 tablespoon apple cider vinegar

1 avocado, peeled, stone removed

1 tablespoon roughly chopped coriander, plus extra leaves to garnish

¼ cup (60 ml) flaxseed oil or hemp seed oil

pinch of Himalayan crystal salt

1 teaspoon roughly chopped garlic

1 stick celery, roughly chopped

¼ teaspoon smoked paprika, plus extra to garnish

½ cup (125 ml) filtered water

4 tomatoes, roughly chopped

6 sundried tomatoes, soaked for 30 minutes and drained

1 cup (150 g) sunflower seeds, soaked for 4 hours in filtered water, then drained, rinsed and roughly chopped

2 corn cobs, kernels removed

Place all the ingredients except the sunflower seeds and corn kernels in a high-powered blender and blend until smooth. Adjust to taste, then stir through the sunflower seeds and corn kernels. Garnish with a sprinkling of extra coriander and smoked paprika.

sprouted quinoa tabbouleh

Sprouted quinoa has a lovely nutty flavour and of course enhances all those wonderful nutrients, as well as making it super-easy to digest. If you are short on time, the same quantity of cooked quinoa will work just as well here. Be sure to soak your quinoa in a bowl of filtered water for a minimum of 10 minutes, then drain before cooking. This is delicious served with hummus (see page 210).

SERVES 4-6

2 cups (320 g) sprouted quinoa (see page 40)

4 spring onions, sliced

handful of mint leaves, torn

handful of coriander leaves, torn, plus extra leaves to garnish

handful of flat-leaf parsley leaves, torn

2 cups (320 g) cherry tomatoes, halved

1 cucumber, seeds removed, diced

1 red capsicum (pepper), seeds and vein removed, diced

2 cloves garlic, minced

½ red onion, thinly sliced

1 tablespoon tamari

DRESSING

½ cup (125 ml) olive oil

½ cup (125 ml) lemon juice

¼ cup (60 ml) apple cider vinegar

pinch of Himalayan crystal salt

1 teaspoon ground cumin

1 teaspoon ground coriander

1 teaspoon ground cinnamon

1 teaspoon caraway seeds

¼ teaspoon smoked paprika

pinch of cayenne pepper

To make the dressing, combine all the ingredients in a high-powered blender. Adjust to taste, then set aside until needed.

Combine all the salad ingredients in a large bowl. Toss through the dressing, then garnish with extra coriander and serve.

vietnamese rice paper rolls with almond dipping sauce

These are an old favourite; even more so when I discovered that kelp noodles make the perfect replacement for traditional rice noodles. So fresh and delicious – ideal for a snack or a party platter. For the dipping sauce, you can buy almond butter from a shop or make it yourself by blitzing almonds in a food processor until they turn into butter.

SERVES 4

12 × 20 cm rice paper wrappers

handful each of coriander, mint and basil leaves

1 cup (80 g) thinly sliced red or green cabbage

170 g chopped kelp noodles (see recipe introduction, page 132)

2 avocados, peeled, stone removed, thinly sliced

2 cups (160 g) bean sprouts

1 yellow capsicum (pepper), seeds and vein removed, julienned

1 cucumber, seeds removed, julienned

1 carrot, julienned

ALMOND DIPPING SAUCE

½ cup (140 g) raw almond butter

⅓ cup (80 ml) filtered water, plus extra if needed

2 tablespoons raw coconut nectar

2 tablespoons apple cider vinegar

2 teaspoons tamari

2 teaspoons finely grated ginger

1 teapsoon finely chopped garlic

pinch of Himalayan crystal salt

To make the dipping sauce, place all the ingredients in a high-powered blender and blend until smooth. Add a little extra water if it is too thick, and adjust the flavour if needed.

Working with one wrapper at a time, dip the wrapper briefly in water then lay flat on a clean surface. Arrange the herbs on the wrapper then layer with a little cabbage, kelp noodles, avocado, bean sprouts and julienned vegetables. Fold the ends in, then roll up and cut in half.

Serve the rice paper rolls with the dipping sauce.

spicy goji, carrot, rocket and fennel salad

This salad has crunch, texture, sweetness and a hint of spice in the creamy mayo. Great to take to work for lunch (keeping the dressing separate) or for impressing friends for a summer get together. The recipe makes more dressing than you'll need for this salad, but I promise you'll have no trouble using it up on other salads or vegetable dishes.

SERVES 4

2 carrots, spiralised

1 bunch rocket

1 bulb fennel, trimmed and thinly sliced

¼ red onion, thinly sliced

½ cup (75 g) hemp or sunflower seeds

½ bunch coriander, torn, plus extra to garnish

½ cup (50 g) goji berries, plus extra to garnish

SPICY MAYO DRESSING

1 cup (150 g) cashews, soaked for 2 hours in filtered water, then rinsed and drained

2 teaspoons curry powder

splash of tamari

¼ teaspoon ground turmeric

½ teaspoon ground cinnamon

¼ teaspoon hot English mustard

1 clove garlic

pinch of cayenne pepper

⅓ cup (40 g) white chia seeds or ¼ cup (50 g) Irish moss paste (see page 26)

½ cup (125 ml) coconut nectar

⅓ cup (80 ml) apple cider vinegar

1 stick celery, thinly sliced

Himalayan crystal salt and ground black pepper

filtered water, for blending

To make the dressing, place all the ingredients in a high-powered blender and blend until smooth. Adjust to taste.

Combine all the salad ingredients in a bowl. Pour the dressing over the salad and toss to coat if desired, then serve garnished with extra goji berries and coriander.

vege medley quiche

I love this hearty dish, and it's wonderfully flexible too. If you don't have a dehydrator, simply marinate the vegetables for 20 minutes and use as they are. If you want to serve the quiche warm, pop it in the dehydrator at 67°C (153°F) for about 20 minutes. Alternatively use the oven method, keeping the temperature below 50°C and the door propped open.

SERVES 8

1 cup (150 g) cashews, soaked for 2 hours in filtered water, then rinsed and drained

2 tablespoons nutritional yeast

1 clove garlic, crushed

juice of 1 lemon

½ cup (125 ml) filtered water, plus extra if needed

splash of tamari

2 tablespoons coconut oil, melted

1 cup (60 g) chopped spinach

1 tablespoon torn basil

micro herbs, to garnish (optional)

MARINATED VEGETABLES

2 tablespoons extra virgin olive oil

¼ cup (60 ml) apple cider vinegar

2 tablespoons raw honey

1 clove garlic, finely chopped

1 tablespoon tamari

2 teaspoons dried Italian herbs

½ cup (30 g) button mushrooms, sliced

½ cup (50 g) sundried tomatoes, soaked for 30 minutes in filtered water, then drained

¼ red capsicum (pepper), seeds and vein removed, thinly sliced

¼ yellow capsicum (pepper), seeds and vein removed, thinly sliced

½ onion, thinly sliced

200 g cherry tomatoes, halved

QUICHE CRUST

¾ cup (120 g) almonds, soaked for 8-12 hours in filtered water, then rinsed and drained

½ cup (75 g) sunflower seeds, soaked for 4 hours in filtered water, then rinsed and drained

2 tablespoons chia seeds

2 tablespoons flaxseed meal

2 tablespoons basil leaves, torn

½ teaspoon Himalayan crystal salt

2 tablespoons coconut oil, melted

To make the marinated vegetables, mix together the olive oil, vinegar, honey, garlic, tamari and mixed herbs and toss through the vegetables. Spread out the vegetable mix on a dehydrator tray lined with baking paper or paraflexx sheets and dehydrate at 48°C (115°F) for 6 hours.

To prepare the crust, spread out the almonds and sunflower seeds on a dehydrator tray lined with baking paper or paraflexx sheets. Dehydrate at 43°C (110°F) for 24 hours.

Place all the crust ingredients in a food processor and blitz until the mixture resembles breadcrumbs. Tip into a 23 cm flan tin and press firmly and evenly over the base. Chill in the fridge while you prepare the filling.

Place the cashews, yeast, garlic, lemon juice, water, tamari and coconut oil in a high-powered blender and blend until smooth. Stir in the spinach, basil and half the marinated vegetables. Pour into the flan tin and place in the fridge for 1-2 hours or until set.

Just before serving, top with the remaining marinated vegetables and micro herbs (if using). Serve warm or at room temperature.

san choy bow

My go-to dish when I'm on the run, this super-healthy version of the traditional san choy bow is guaranteed to become a family favourite. To make the lettuce cups, gently peel the lettuce leaves away from the core – you can trim the edges to make a neat circular shape if you like.

SERVES 4

12 iceberg lettuce cups

sliced spring onion and sesame seeds, to serve

MARINADE

1 tablespoon sesame oil

2 tablespoons tamari

2 tablespoons lime juice

1 small red chilli, seeded and finely chopped

1 tablespoon raw coconut nectar

pinch of Himalayan crystal salt

FILLING

100 g swiss brown mushrooms, finely diced

2 teaspoons grated ginger

1 clove garlic, crushed

1 red capsicum (pepper), seeds and vein removed, finely diced

10 cm piece of daikon (mooli), peeled and finely diced

2 spring onions, thinly sliced

1 cup (100 g) walnuts, soaked for 4 hours in filtered water, then rinsed, drained and roughly chopped

2 corn cobs, kernels removed

1 cup (100 g) green beans, sliced

½ bunch coriander, roughly chopped

½ bunch mint, roughly chopped

To make the marinade, combine all the ingredients in a bowl.

For the filling, place all the ingredients in a large bowl. Pour over the marinade and stir to combine, then set aside for 10 minutes.

Spoon the filling into the lettuce cups and garnish with spring onion and a sprinkling of sesame seeds. Roll up and eat!

sushi

The spice paste adds a fantastic hit of flavour to these fresh rolls, but are you can make them without it if you prefer. Just add extra vegetables of your choice.

SERVES 4

4 sheets nori

4 large (or 8 small) lettuce leaves

1 cup (200 g) sushi rice (see page 213)

½ red capsicum (pepper), seeds and vein removed, cut into thin strips

1 small carrot, cut into thin strips

1 cucumber, cut into thin strips

½ avocado, thinly sliced

1 mango, thinly sliced (optional)

1 cup (40 g) alfalfa sprouts

tamari, to serve

SPICE PASTE

½ cup (140 g) tahini

2 tablespoons white miso paste

1 teaspoon sesame oil

¼ teaspoon cayenne pepper

1 small red chilli, seeded

2 teaspoons ground turmeric

pinch of Himalayan crystal salt

⅓ cup (80 ml) apple cider vinegar

2½–3 tablespoons coconut sugar

filtered water, if needed

To prepare the spice paste, place all the ingredients in a high-powered blender and blend to a smooth paste. Add a little water if necessary and adjust to taste. Store in an airtight container in the fridge for up to 1 week. Makes about 1 cup (280 g).

To assemble, place the nori sheets on a board, shiny-side down, and top with the lettuce. Spread 1–2 teaspoons of the spice paste over the lettuce and gently flatten it down. Spoon ¼ cup (50 g) of the sushi rice across each sheet about a third of the way up, then arrange the vegetables, mango (if using) and sprouts alongside. Roll up and seal the edges with water. Cut into even pieces and serve with a bowl of tamari, for dipping.

green and red tomato corn soup

Heart-friendly soup! Tomatoes, especially when blended, are high in lycopene, a potent antioxidant that plays an important role in reducing cardiovascular risk. If you can't find green tomatoes, experiment with heirloom tomatoes or kumatos.

SERVES 4

2 corn cobs, kernels removed

½ red capsicum (pepper), seeds and vein removed, diced

½ yellow capsicum (pepper), seeds and vein removed, diced

½ green capsicum (pepper), seeds and vein removed, diced

1 red tomato, diced

1 green tomato, diced

1 large avocado, peeled, stone removed, diced, plus extra to serve

2 sticks celery, finely diced

2 tablespoons apple cider vinegar

2 spring onions, thinly sliced

2 tablespoons olive oil

½ bunch basil, roughly chopped

½ bunch coriander, roughly chopped, plus extra leaves to serve

Himalayan crystal salt and ground black pepper

SOUP BASE

4 large red tomatoes

4 large green tomatoes

1 tablespoon white miso paste

1 clove garlic

To make the soup base, place all the ingredients in a food processor and process until smooth.

Pour the base into a large bowl and stir in the remaining ingredients. Season to taste and serve, topped with extra avocado and coriander leaves.

coconut wraps with hummus and falafel

The coconut wraps are delicious and once dehydrated will last for months in the fridge. However, if you are short on time or don't have a dehydrator you can use collard greens or large cos lettuce leaves as alternative wraps. Fillings can also vary – get creative! Think spinach, rocket, grated carrot or beetroot, tomato, avocado, sprouts, marinated vegetables, lemon tahini dressing (see page 221) or nut cheese (see page 207). Yum!

SERVES 4

flesh of 4–5 young coconuts, reserving the coconut water

Himalayan crystal salt and ground white pepper

2 teaspoons psyllium husk powder

your choice of salad greens and vegetables, to serve

cashew hummus (see page 210), for spreading

FALAFEL

1 cup (160 g) almonds

½ cup (50 g) walnuts, soaked for 4 hours in filtered water, then rinsed and drained

¼ white onion

1 clove garlic

¼ cup (70 g) tahini

1 tablespoon lemon juice

1 tablespoon olive oil

handful of flat-leaf parsley leaves

handful of coriander leaves

1 teaspoon ground cumin

1 teaspoon Himalayan crystal salt

sesame seeds, for rolling

Place the coconut flesh and enough coconut water to cover in a high-powered blender and blend until it reaches the consistency of a batter. Add more coconut water if needed, and season with salt and pepper. Just before dehydrating, stir in the psyllium husk. Spread out the mixture on two dehydrator trays lined with baking paper or paraflexx sheets to a thickness of about 3 mm, pushing it right to the edges. Dehydrate at 43°C (110°F) for 1 hour, then score each batch into four squares and continue to dehydrate for a further 3–4 hours.

For the falafel, place the almonds in a heatproof bowl. Pour boiling water over the nuts, then leave for 10 minutes. Slip off the skins. Place in a food processor with the remaining ingredients (except the sesame seeds) process until combined. Adjust to taste. Form tablespoons of the mixture into balls (there should be enough to make about 16 balls) and roll in the sesame seeds to coat. Serve as is or dehydrate at 43°C (110°F) for 8 hours. Once dehydrated these will keep for a month in an airtight container in the fridge. They also freeze really well.

To assemble, place the coconut wraps on a board and top with your choice of greens and vegetables. Top with the falafels and hummus. Fold the sides in and roll up firmly, enclosing the filling ingredients as you go.

minted pea salad with coconut bacon

I really look forward to making this in spring and summer. This refreshing salad is topped with healthy, cruelty-free bacon. You can also add a mixed nut topping of your choice or a good handful of chopped kale for extra protein, fibre and goodness.

SERVES 4

2 cups (320 g) podded peas
(or frozen peas, thawed)

100 g snowpeas (mange-tout), sliced

2 avocados, peeled, stone removed, sliced

handful of snowpea sprouts

2 handfuls of mint leaves, roughly chopped

⅓ cup (20 g) coconut bacon
(see page 209)

fermented nut cheese (see page 207), to serve (optional)

ground black pepper

DRESSING

2 tablespoons extra virgin olive oil

2 tablespoons lemon juice

1 small golden shallot, finely diced

1 clove garlic, crushed

1 tablespoon raw coconut nectar

½ teaspoon hot English mustard

pinch of Himalayan crystal salt

To make the dressing, place all the ingredients in a glass jar and shake to combine.

Place the peas, snowpeas, avocado, sprouts and mint in a large bowl, add the dressing and toss gently to coat. Sprinkle with the coconut bacon and nut cheese (if using), finish with a grinding of pepper and serve.

zucchini pasta with broad beans, asparagus and peas in a light cashew cream sauce

I love this light, summery dish. To maintain the integrity of the sauce with the pasta, dress the pasta just before serving. If you are short of time you don't have to salt the zucchini: just spiralise and go.

SERVES 4

1 cup (100 g) walnuts, soaked for 4 hours in filtered water, then rinsed, drained and roughly chopped

2 cups (240 g) peeled broad beans

1 bunch asparagus, cut into 3 cm pieces

⅔ cup (110 g) podded peas (or frozen peas, thawed)

small handful of coconut bacon (see page 209)

small handful of parmesan (see page 206)

roughly chopped basil or mint leaves, to serve (optional)

CASHEW CREAM SAUCE

1 cup (150 g) cashews, soaked for 2 hours in filtered water, then rinsed and drained

¾ cup (185 ml) filtered water, plus extra if needed

1 clove garlic, crushed

1½ tablespoons nutritional yeast

1 tablespoon lemon juice

1 tablespoon white miso paste

Himalayan crystal salt

ZUCCHINI PASTA

8 medium zucchini (courgettes)

⅛ teaspoon mineral salt

filtered water, for rinsing

To make the cashew cream sauce, place all the ingredients in a food processor or high-powered blender and process until smooth. If it is too thick add a little more water. Adjust to taste.

For the zucchini pasta, peel the zucchini and chop the ends off, then create spaghetti using a vege spiraliser. Place in a bowl and mix through the salt. Allow to sit for 10 minutes, then drain and rinse with filtered water, and squeeze out any excess moisture.

Place the walnuts, broad beans, asparagus, peas and pasta in a large bowl. Add enough cashew sauce to coat and gently stir to combine. Serve topped with coconut bacon, parmesan and chopped herbs, if using.

Note

To make this recipe completely sugar free, replace the coconut nectar in the dressing with 3 drops of stevia liquid.

roasted vegetable salad with spinach, quinoa and poppy seeds

This wonderfully hearty vegan dish is great for cold winter days or for when you just feel like something cooked.

SERVES 4

500 g pumpkin (squash), peeled and cut into 3 cm pieces

2 zucchini (courgettes), cut into 3 cm pieces

200 g brussels sprouts, halved or 1 large beetroot, peeled and cut into wedges

1 large red onion, peeled and cut into wedges

1 red capsicum (pepper), seeds and vein removed, cut into large pieces

¼ cup (50 g) coconut oil, melted

Himalayan crystal salt and ground black pepper

1 cup (190 g) quinoa, soaked for 10 minutes in filtered water, rinsed

2 cups (500 ml) filtered water

2 large handfuls of baby spinach

½ pomegranate, seeds removed

¼ cup (35 g) sunflower seeds

2 tablespoons poppy seeds

DRESSING

1 tablespoon apple cider vinegar

1 tablespoon tahini

1 tablespoon extra virgin olive oil

1 tablespoon lemon juice

6 drops of stevia liquid, or to taste

pinch of Himalayan crystal salt

Preheat the oven to 190°C (375°F). Line two baking trays with baking paper.

Arrange the pumpkin, zucchini, brussels sprouts or beetroot, onion and capsicum on the prepared trays. Drizzle with coconut oil and season with salt and pepper, then roast for 35–40 minutes or until cooked. Keep an eye on the onion and capsicum – you may need to remove them earlier.

Meanwhile, place the quinoa and water in a medium saucepan and bring to the boil. Reduce the heat and cook, covered, for 15–20 minutes or until all the water has been absorbed.

To make the dressing, place all the ingredients in a glass jar and shake to combine.

Place the roasted vegetables and quinoa in a large bowl. Add the dressing and spinach and stir to combine. Top with the pomegranate, sunflower and poppy seeds, season to taste and serve immediately.

coconut fennel noodles with sauerkraut and red cabbage

The sweetness and creaminess of the coconut makes this dish very special. Topping it off with sauerkraut will help with digestion and give you a boost of good bacteria.

SERVES 4

1 large bulb fennel, trimmed and thinly sliced

flesh of 1 young coconut, thinly sliced

1 parsnip, spiralised

¼ red cabbage, shredded

1 white onion, thinly sliced

1 tablespoon finely chopped dill

large handful of coriander leaves, plus extra to garnish

a splash of lemon tahini dressing (see page 221)

1 cup (100 g) sauerkraut (see page 214)

black sesame seeds, to garnish

Combine the fennel, coconut, parsnip, cabbage, onion, dill and coriander in a large bowl. Toss through the dressing, then top with the sauerkraut and extra coriander and garnish with a sprinkling of sesame seeds.

shredded beetroot and daikon salad with pesto

The healthful combination of liver-loving beetroot and detoxifying pesto is tasty medicine on a plate!

SERVES 4

⅓ cup (50 g) pumpkin seeds, soaked for 4–6 hours in filtered water, then rinsed and drained and roughly chopped

⅓ cup (50 g) sunflower seeds, soaked for 4 hours in filtered water, then rinsed and drained

4 medium beetroot, peeled and spiralised or coarsely grated

½ daikon (mooli), peeled and spiralised or coarsely grated

8 radishes, thinly sliced

large handful of flat-leaf parsley leaves

½ cup (130 g) pesto (see page 216), plus extra to serve (optional)

Spread out the pumpkin seeds and sunflower seeds on a dehydrator tray lined with baking paper or paraflexx sheets. Dehydrate at 43°C (110°F) for 12–24 hours.

Place the beetroot, daikon, radish and parsley in a bowl, add the pesto and mix together well. Sprinkle with pumpkin and sunflower seeds and finish with an extra dollop of pesto, if liked.

rocket, avocado and tomato salad with pomegranate and mint

The peppery bite of rocket combined with creamy avocado and tart bursts of pomegranate make this salad a winner!

SERVES 4

400 g mixed small tomatoes, halved (or quartered if large)

1 golden shallot, finely chopped

1 clove garlic, crushed

1 tablespoon extra virgin olive oil

1 tablespoon apple cider vinegar

2 teaspoons raw coconut nectar

Himalayan crystal salt and ground black pepper

150 g baby rocket

1 avocado, peeled, stone removed, diced

½ pomegranate, seeds removed

handful of mint leaves

DRESSING

2 tablespoons extra virgin olive oil

1 tablespoon apple cider vinegar

1 teaspoon finely chopped mint

Himalayan crystal salt

Combine the tomato, shallot, garlic, olive oil, vinegar, coconut nectar, salt and pepper in a bowl and set aside for 20 minutes.

To make the dressing, place all the ingredients in a glass jar and shake to combine.

Place the tomato mixture, rocket and avocado in a large bowl, add the dressing and gently toss to coat. Top with the pomegranate seeds and mint leaves and serve.

carrot, arame and kale salad with sweet soy and spicy seed mix

The sweetness of the carrot and the subtle sea-vegetable flavour of the arame combined with crunchy seeds and liver-loving kale make this salad irresistible! Definitely one of my favourites.

SERVES 4

½ bunch kale, hard stalks removed, leaves finely shredded

2 carrots, grated

2 tablespoons arame, soaked for 10 minutes in filtered water, then rinsed and drained

1 Lebanese cucumber, seeded and cut into thin sticks

handful of coriander leaves

handful of basil leaves, torn

spicy seed mix (see page 152), for sprinkling

SWEET SOY DRESSING

2 tablespoons tamari

1 tablespoon flaxseed oil or extra virgin olive oil

1 tablespoon apple cider vinegar

2 cm piece of ginger, finely grated

2 tablespoons raw coconut nectar

To make the dressing, place all the ingredients in a glass jar and shake to combine. Adjust to taste.

Place the kale in a large bowl and add the dressing, then use your hands to rub the dressing into the leaves. Add the carrot, arame, cucumber and herbs and gently toss to combine.

Serve sprinkled with spicy seed mix.

ner

chapter

spicy tahini sweet potato pasta

This is a quick and easy dish to make and so colourful! If preferred, you can replace the sweet potato with zucchini, parsnip, beetroot or carrot, or a combination of all for a complete rainbow meal!

SERVES 4

700 g sweet potato, spiralised

4 tomatoes, seeded and diced

½ bunch kale, finely chopped

1 cup (140 g) roughly chopped cashews or other nuts of your choice, plus extra to garnish

½ red onion, thinly sliced

handful of basil leaves, very thinly sliced, plus extra to garnish (optional)

⅓ cup (90 g) tahini

2 teaspoons raw coconut nectar

½ cup (125 ml) olive oil

1 clove garlic, minced

¼ teaspoon cayenne pepper

2 tablespoons nutritional yeast

pinch of Himalayan crystal salt

2 tablespoons lemon juice

2 tablespoons apple cider vinegar

Place the sweet potato, tomato, kale, cashews, onion and basil in a large bowl and toss to combine.

Blitz the remaining ingredients in a mini blender until smooth and combined. Adjust to taste.

Massage the tahini sauce into the vegetable mixture, garnish with extra cashews and basil sprigs (if liked) and serve.

miso broth with sprouted quinoa

Unpasteurised miso paste is very delicate and precious enzymes will be destroyed if this is served too hot, so it's important you use hot but not boiling water here. If you are short on time you could cook the quinoa instead of sprouting it, or omit it altogether.

SERVES 2

⅓ cup (55 g) brown rice miso paste

1 cup (60 g) mushrooms, sliced

2 handfuls of baby spinach

1 carrot, thinly sliced

¼ head broccoli, cut into small florets

½ cup (50 g) green beans, cut into 1 cm pieces

1 clove garlic, minced

1 cm piece of ginger, minced

2½–3 tablespoons chopped coriander, plus extra leaves to garnish

2 umeboshi plums, chopped

2 tablespoons coconut oil, melted

1 tablespoon arame or hijiki seaweed

1–2 cups (160–320 g) sprouted quinoa (see page 40)

Divide all the ingredients evenly between two bowls.

Bring a jug of water to the boil. Wait 5 minutes, then pour 2 cups (500 ml) hot water into the bowls and stir until the miso paste has dissolved. Garnish with extra coriander leaves and serve immediately.

beetroot and mushroom ravioli with pesto

The vibrant colour of the beetroot really pops with the pesto in this beautiful-looking dish, inspired by Seeds of Life cafe in Ubud, Bali. The earthy tones of the filling come through thanks to the mushroom, walnut and a subtle hint of truffle. This also makes a great entree if you're entertaining, and I also like to keep a few on hand to eat as a snack.

SERVES 4

2 large beetroot, thinly sliced

2 tablespoons olive oil

Himalayan crystal salt

⅓ cup (90 g) pesto (see page 216)

micro herbs and watercress dressed with olive oil and apple cider vinegar, to serve

FILLING

½ cup (50 g) walnuts, soaked for 4 hours in filtered water, then rinsed and drained

80 g swiss brown mushrooms, roughly chopped

¾ cup (150 g) fermented nut cheese (see page 207)

1 teaspoon chopped basil

1 tablespoon olive oil

1 tablespoon truffle oil (optional)

2 teaspoons lemon juice

Himalayan crystal salt and ground black pepper

Toss the beetroot with the olive oil and a little salt. Set aside.

To make the filling, pulse the walnuts and mushrooms in a food processor to form a coarse 'mince'. Add the remaining ingredients and pulse again. Adjust to taste.

Place four slices of beetroot on each plate and spoon 2–3 teaspoons of filling onto each one. Top each ravioli with another slice of beetroot and press gently. Dollop a teaspoon of pesto onto each ravioli and serve with the dressed micro herbs and watercress.

mushroom burgers

Oh so easy and oh so good! If you have prepared fermented nut cheese ahead of time, it goes wonderfully well with this dish. Don't worry if not – it will still be delicious.

SERVES 4

⅓ cup (80 ml) tamari

⅓ cup (80 ml) olive oil, plus extra to serve

juice of ½ lemon

1 clove garlic, minced

8 large portobello mushrooms, stems removed

fermented nut cheese (see page 207), to serve (optional)

VEGE COMBO TOPPING

100 g baby spinach

⅔ cup (110 g) cherry tomatoes, quartered

½ red capsicum (pepper), seeds and vein removed, sliced

2 tablespoons thinly sliced basil

handful of green beans, diced

1 corn cob, kernels removed

⅓ cup (50 g) pine nuts

1 teaspoon onion powder

½ teaspoon garlic powder

1 avocado, peeled, stone removed, diced

¼ cup (60 ml) flaxseed oil

2 teaspoons raw honey

2 teaspoons tamari

2 teaspoons apple cider vinegar

Combine the tamari, olive oil, lemon juice and garlic in a bowl, add the mushrooms and toss to coat. Place the mushrooms on a dehydrator tray lined with baking paper or paraflexx sheets and dehydrate at 43°C (110°F) for 2–4 hours. Remove and set aside. If you don't have a dehydrator you can just marinate the mushrooms for 20 minutes.

To make the topping, place all the ingredients in a bowl and toss to combine.

To assemble, place half the mushrooms on serving plates, bottom-side up, and spread with a layer of fermented cheese (if using). Pile the vege combo over the cheese, then place another mushroom on top to create a 'burger'. Finish with a drizzle of olive oil and serve.

mega vege pizzas

Who doesn't love pizza? Now you can relax and enjoy a gluten-free, guilt-free pizza that tastes amazing! The pizza bases freeze really well so make them in bulk so you always have some on hand.

SERVES 4

1 tablespoon olive oil

pinch of Himalayan crystal salt

1 teaspoon tamari

1 teaspoon raw honey

½ cup (40 g) small broccoli florets

1 zucchini (courgette), sliced

1 cup (260 g) marinara sauce (see page 226)

1 red capsicum (pepper), vein and seeds removed, julienned

handful of mushrooms, sliced

½ red onion, sliced

handful of cherry tomatoes, quartered or halved

1 avocado, peeled, stone removed, sliced

handful of olives, sliced or torn

fresh herbs, to garnish

2 handfuls of rocket

PIZZA BASES

1 cup (100 g) walnuts, soaked for 4 hours in filtered water, then rinsed and drained

1 zucchini (courgette), peeled and roughly chopped

1 cup (100 g) roughly chopped cauliflower

1 cup (135 g) peeled, roughly chopped pumpkin (squash)

½ cup (125 ml) hemp seed oil or olive oil

¼ cup (60 ml) lemon juice

pinch of Himalayan crystal salt

1 cup (95 g) flaxseed meal

To make the pizza bases, place all the ingredients except the flaxseed meal in a high-powered blender and blend until smooth. Pour into a bowl and stir through the flaxseed meal. Spread out the mixture on a dehydrator tray lined with baking paper or paraflexx sheets to form into four small rounds or two large rounds. Dehydrate at 43°C (110°F) for 4 hours. Remove the baking paper or paraflexx sheets from the tray and dehydrate the pizza bases for another 8–10 hours or until firm.

Combine the olive oil, salt, tamari and honey in a bowl, add the broccoli and zucchini and toss to coat. Set aside to marinate for 20–30 minutes.

Spread the marinara sauce over the pizza bases and top with the marinated vegetables and remaining ingredients. Scatter with rocket and serve. This is best served when the pizza bases are still warm from the dehydrator.

raw pad thai with kaffir lime

This wonderfully fresh summer dish is so much better than the carbohydrate-laden original. I promise you'll love it.

SERVES 4

handful each of bean sprouts, mint, Thai basil and coriander leaves

handful of chopped nuts (such as macadamias or cashews)

1 long red chilli, seeded and thinly sliced

lime wedges, to serve

SAUCE

1 cup (150 g) cashews, soaked for 2 hours in filtered water, then rinsed and drained

1 tablespoon dulse flakes

1 clove garlic, crushed

1 teaspoon grated ginger

1 small red chilli, seeded and roughly chopped

1 stem lemongrass, white part only, roughly chopped

finely grated zest of 1 lime

¼ cup (60 ml) lime juice

2 tablespoons tamari

6 kaffir lime leaves, roughly chopped

1 teaspoon raw coconut nectar

¼ cup (60 ml) filtered water, plus extra if needed

½ teaspoon Himalayan crystal salt, or to taste

2 tablespoons olive oil

NOODLES

2–3 large zucchini (courgettes), spiralised

1 large carrot, spiralised

½ red onion, thinly sliced

1 cup (80 g) thinly sliced cabbage

handful of snowpeas (mange-tout), thinly sliced

½ red capsicum (pepper), seeds and vein removed, thinly sliced

1½ cups (120 g) bean sprouts

handful of Thai basil leaves (or basil)

handful of mint leaves

handful of coriander leaves

To prepare the sauce, place all the ingredients except the olive oil in a high-powered blender and blend until smooth and creamy. Add the olive oil and blend again. Set aside.

Combine all the ingredients for the noodles in a large bowl, add the sauce and gently toss to coat. Serve topped with bean sprouts, fresh herbs, chopped nuts and chilli, with lime wedges on the side.

asian stir-fry with spicy cashews and kelp noodles

This is one of my favourite quick meals – it's sooo tasty, with the added benefit of arame seaweed, making it high in trace minerals, calcium and iodine. Kelp noodles are calorie free and carbohydrate free and so easy to use: simply remove them from the packet, rinse and drain, and then cut to the desired size. You can buy them online or from health-food stores.

SERVES 4

kelp noodles, to serve

handful of herbs (such as basil, coriander and/or mint), torn

SPICY CASHEWS

1 cup (150 g) cashews, soaked for 2 hours in filtered water, then rinsed and drained

½ teaspoon ground star anise

½ teaspoon Chinese five-spice powder

1 teaspoon dried chilli flakes

½ teaspoon Himalayan crystal salt

1 teaspoon ground ginger

1 teaspoon garlic powder

1 teaspoon onion powder

juice of ½ lime

splash of olive oil

SAUCE

¼ cup (60 ml) olive oil

2 medjool dates, pitted

finely grated zest and juice of 1 lime

1 clove garlic, crushed

3 teaspoons grated ginger

¼ cup (60 ml) tamari

1 small red chilli, seeded and chopped

2 tablespoons raw coconut nectar

⅓ cup (80 ml) sesame oil

STIR-FRY VEGETABLES

handful of snowpeas (mange-tout), thinly sliced

handful of green beans, cut into 3 cm pieces

1 carrot, cut into thin sticks

4 baby corn, quartered

2 zucchini (courgettes), cut into thin sticks

1 red capsicum (pepper), seeds and vein removed, thinly sliced

¼ Chinese cabbage, thinly sliced

1 cup (90 g) mushrooms, thinly sliced

½ red onion, thinly sliced

2 tablespoons arame or wakame seaweed, soaked for 10 minutes in filtered water, then rinsed and drained

To prepare the spicy cashews, combine all the ingredients in a large bowl. Spread out the mixture on a dehydrator tray lined with baking paper or paraflexx sheets and dehydrate at 43°C (110°F) for 6–8 hours or until dried. Roughly chop the nuts and set aside.

To make the sauce, place all the ingredients in a high-powered blender and blend until smooth. Adjust the flavour balance to taste.

Place all the stir-fry vegetables in a bowl, pour over the sauce and massage through the vegetables. If you want a softer finish to your dish, leave them to marinate for 10 minutes before serving. This will soften up the veges and give them a cooked texture.

Divide the stir-fry vegetables and kelp noodles among four bowls and sprinkle the spicy cashews and fresh herbs over the top. Pour over any remaining sauce if there is any and serve.

shepherd's pie with sweet potato mash

Sweet potatoes are a great source of Vitamin A, C, B1, B2 and B6. They are also high in fibre and minerals and fun to work with raw. This nourishing pie may be served at room temperature or warmed through in the dehydrator – just the thing for when you feel like something hearty.

SERVES 4

2 cups (200 g) walnuts, soaked for 4 hours in filtered water, then rinsed and drained

½ cup (75 g) sunflower seeds, soaked for 4 hours in filtered water, then rinsed and drained

1 clove garlic

1 cup (90 g) diced mushrooms

1 zucchini (courgette), roughly chopped

½ cup (50 g) sundried tomatoes, soaked for 30 minutes, drained and chopped

3 roma (plum) tomatoes, seeded and roughly chopped

3 medjool dates, pitted

2 tablespoons oregano leaves, plus extra to garnish

2 tablespoons apple cider vinegar

2 tablespoons tamari

1 teaspoon onion powder

½ teaspoon Himalayan crystal salt, or to taste

ground black pepper, to garnish

SWEET POTATO MASH

½ cup (75 g) cashews, soaked for 2 hours in filtered water, then rinsed and drained

300 g sweet potato, cut into chunks

300 g cauliflower florets, roughly broken

2 tablespoons nutritional yeast

2 tablespoons olive oil

1 tablespoon white miso paste

1 teaspoon garlic powder

3–4 drops of stevia liquid, or to taste

½ teaspoon Himalayan crystal salt, or to taste

Place the walnuts, sunflower seeds and garlic in a food processor and process until coarsely chopped. Add the remaining ingredients (except the garnishes) and process to a 'mince' texture. Spoon into a 1.5 litre baking dish.

To prepare the sweet potato mash, combine all the ingredients in a food processor until very finely chopped and the consistency of mash. Spoon over the 'mince', garnish with extra oregano leaves and a few grindings of pepper and serve.

spicy nachos

This is a firm favourite with everyone I serve it to. It's the healthiest version of nachos around – a great substitute for when the Mexican craving hits and well worth the effort. If you don't have time to make your own corn chips you can buy organic regular or blue corn chips. Delicious!

SERVES 4-6

corn chips (see page 154), cashew sour cream (see page 208) and mashed avocado, to serve

coriander leaves and lime wedges, to garnish

'MEAT'

1½ cups (150 g) walnuts, soaked for 4 hours in filtered water, then rinsed and drained

½ cup (75 g) sunflower seeds, soaked for 4 hours in filtered water, then rinsed and drained

2 tomatoes, seeded and diced

½ red capsicum (pepper), seeds and vein removed, finely diced

1 carrot, finely diced

1 zucchini (courgette), diced

1 cup (90 g) finely diced mushrooms

½ red onion, finely diced

2 tablespoons chopped coriander

2 tablespoons tamari

2 tablespoons lemon juice

1 clove garlic, crushed

¼ teaspoon cayenne pepper

¼ teaspoon smoked paprika

1 tablespoon Mexican chilli powder (adjust to your level of spiciness)

2 teaspoons dried chilli flakes

1 teaspoon Himalayan crystal salt

To make the 'meat', place the walnuts and sunflower seeds in a food processor and process until crumbly. Tip into a bowl and add the remaining ingredients. Spread out the mixture on a dehydrator tray lined with baking paper or paraflexx sheets and dehydrate at 48°C (115°F) for 2–4 hours until softened but still juicy. Transfer to a bowl and store in the fridge until needed – it will keep for up to 5 days.

To assemble, arrange the corn chips on a large plate and top with the 'meat' and a large dollop of cashew sour cream. Finish with mashed avocado, fresh coriander and lime wedges.

curried vegetable patties with slaw and minty coconut yoghurt

This is a lovely cooked dish with a hint of Indian flavours. Don't be put off by the length of the ingredients list – it all comes together surprisingly quickly. The patties freeze really well or may be stored in the fridge for up to 5 days.

SERVES 4

1 zucchini (courgette), grated

1 small carrot, grated

½ small sweet potato, peeled and grated

½ small celeriac, grated

2 spring onions, thinly sliced

1 clove garlic, crushed

1 teaspoon grated ginger

3 teaspoons curry powder

½ cup (75 g) buckwheat flour

1 teaspoon Himalayan crystal salt

coconut oil, for pan-frying

MINTY COCONUT YOGHURT

1 cup (280 g) coconut yoghurt (see page 212)

handful of mint leaves, finely chopped

Himalayan crystal salt

SLAW

⅛ red cabbage, finely shredded

⅛ green cabbage, finely shredded

2 tablespoons arame, soaked for 10 minutes in filtered water, then rinsed and drained

1 small red onion, thinly sliced

2 handfuls of coriander leaves

2 handfuls of mint leaves

¼ cup (25 g) goji berries

DRESSING

2 tablespoons extra virgin olive oil

1 clove garlic, crushed

2 tablespoons lime juice

2 teaspoons raw coconut nectar

¼ teaspoon cayenne pepper

½ teaspoon ground cumin

½ teaspoon ground coriander

½ teaspoon Himalayan crystal salt

To make the minty coconut yoghurt, combine all the ingredients in a small bowl.

For the slaw, place all the ingredients in a large bowl.

To make the dressing, place all the ingredients in a glass jar and shake to combine. Add to the slaw and gently toss to coat.

Place the grated vegetables, spring onion, garlic, ginger, curry powder, flour and salt in a large bowl and mix together well using your hands. Heat a little coconut oil in a large frying pan (you may need to use two) over medium heat. Add mounds of about ½ cup of the patty mixture and gently flatten with a spatula (you should have enough mixture to make eight patties). Cook for 3–4 minutes each side or until golden.

Serve the patties with the minted yoghurt and slaw.

vegetable moussaka

Another hearty dish for those craving their old favourites, but in a healthier form. All this satisfying dish needs is a simple green salad to go with it, although the sprouted quinoa tabbouleh (page 88) also works beautifully. This can also be made with thin strips of peeled raw zucchini (courgette).

SERVES 4

2 large eggplants (aubergines)

Himalayan crystal salt, for sprinkling

2 tablespoons olive oil

¼ cup (60 ml) lemon juice

1 teaspoon Himalayan crystal salt, extra

2 cups (520 g) marinara sauce (see page 226)

'MEAT'

1 cup (100 g) walnuts, soaked for 4 hours in filtered water, then rinsed and drained

2 tomatoes, seeded and chopped

75 g mushrooms

½ red onion

1 garlic clove

1 tablespoon tamari

1 tablespoon lemon juice

1 tablespoon oregano leaves

2–3 drops of stevia liquid

CHEESE SAUCE

1 cup (150 g) cashews, soaked for 2 hours in filtered water, then rinsed and drained

1 clove garlic

1 tablespoon nutritional yeast

2 teaspoons lemon juice

Himalayan crystal salt and ground white pepper

¼–½ cup (60–125 ml) filtered water or nut milk (see page 204)

Thinly slice the eggplants, then sprinkle generously with salt and set aside for 30 minutes. Rinse and drain well. Combine the olive oil, lemon juice and extra salt in a large bowl, add the eggplant and turn to coat, then set aside for 1 hour. Remove the eggplant from the marinade and arrange on a dehydrator tray lined with baking paper or paraflexx sheets. Dehydrate at 43°C (110°F) for 4 hours or until soft.

To prepare the 'meat', place all the ingredients in a food processor and process to the texture of mince. Spread out the mixture on a dehydrator tray lined with baking paper or paraflexx sheets and dehydrate at 43°C (110°F) for 4 hours.

For the cheese sauce, place all the ingredients in a food processor and process until smooth, adding as much liquid as necessary to form a pouring consistency.

Line the base of a 28 cm × 10 cm loaf tin or a 20 cm square dish with baking paper. Place slices of eggplant to form a layer over the base then top with the the marinara sauce. Repeat with another layer of eggplant, followed by the 'meat', pressing down gently to ensure there are no gaps. For best results, place in the fridge for 2 hours or until ready to serve. Turn out of the tin or dish and cut into portions, then spoon the cheese sauce over the top and serve.

fried rice with sweet soy sauce

This can be served in so many ways – a generous bowlful makes a terrific main course, but it also works as a light lunch and may be offered as a lovely side dish.

SERVES 4

½ medium cauliflower, broken into florets

3 spring onions, thinly sliced

1 clove garlic, crushed

1 teaspoon grated ginger

1 small red chilli, seeded and finely chopped

1 stick celery, finely diced

1 corn cob, kernels removed

1 cup (160 g) cherry tomatoes, quartered

100 g podded peas (or frozen peas, thawed)

50 g mushrooms, finely diced

large handful of bean sprouts, plus extra to serve

handful of coriander leaves, finely chopped, plus extra to serve

handful of flat-leaf parsley or mint leaves, finely chopped

large handful of coconut bacon (see page 209)

handful of chopped cashews

lime wedges, to serve (optional)

SWEET SOY SAUCE

⅓ cup (80 ml) tamari

1 tablespoon apple cider vinegar

2 tablespoons seasme oil

1 tablespoon raw honey

To make the sweet soy sauce, combine all the ingredients in a small high-powered blender. Adjust to taste and set aside.

Place the cauliflower florets in a food processor and pulse to the texture of rice. Tip into a large bowl, add the remaining vegetables, sprouts, herbs, coconut bacon and half the sweet soy sauce and mix together well.

Scatter with extra sprouts, coriander and cashews, then serve with lime wedges (if using) and the remaining sweet soy sauce on the side.

stir-fried broccolini and asparagus with millet

A favourite option of mine when I feel like a lightly cooked meal, this brilliant vegan dish is so good for you. Millet is a wonderful creamy gluten-free grain, perfect for a stir-fry.

SERVES 4

1 cup (200 g) millet, rinsed

2 cups (500 ml) filtered water, plus extra if needed

2 tablespoons coconut oil, melted

1 red onion, thinly sliced

1 clove garlic, crushed

2 bunches broccolini, halved

1 bunch asparagus, trimmed and halved

1 red capsicum (pepper), seeds and vein removed, sliced

100 g button mushrooms, halved

1 teaspoon smoked paprika

¼ cup (60 ml) lemon juice

1 teaspoon raw honey or raw coconut nectar

1 tablespoon tahini

Himalayan crystal salt

handful flat-leaf parsley leaves, plus extra to serve

chopped red chilli, to serve (optional)

Place the millet and water in a saucepan and bring to the boil, then reduce the heat and simmer for 20 minutes or until all the water has been absorbed.

Heat the coconut oil in a wok or large frying pan over medium heat, add the onion and cook until translucent. Add the garlic and cook for 1 minute. Add the remaining vegetables and stir-fry for 4–5 minutes or until just cooked.

Reduce the heat to low. Stir through the paprika, lemon juice, honey or coconut nectar, tahini, salt and parsley. Adjust to taste, then divide among four bowls, top with extra parsley and chilli (if using) and serve with the millet on the side.

quinoa and vege stir-fry

This dish is so flexible, it's more of a guide than a hard-and-fast recipe. It's an ideal way of using up leftover vegetables, and you can even add leftover tomato sauces if you like. Save this for when you're having a mini-break from raw.

SERVES 4

½ cup (95 g) quinoa, soaked for 10 minutes in filtered water, rinsed

1 cup (250 ml) filtered water

2 tablespoons coconut oil

1 onion, thinly sliced

2 cloves garlic, thinly sliced

1 large red chilli, seeded and finely chopped

6 cups mixed vegetables, such as thinly sliced carrot or celery, broccoli florets, Chinese broccoli, mushrooms or sliced zucchini (courgette) or capsicum (pepper)

filtered water, extra, if needed

your choice of fresh herbs, to garnish

SAUCE
¼ cup (60 ml) tamari

2 tablespoons lemon juice

1 tablespoon raw honey

½ teaspoon Himalayan crystal salt

Place the quinoa and water in a medium saucepan and bring to the boil. Reduce the heat and cook, covered, for 15–20 minutes or until all the water has been absorbed.

To make the sauce, combine all the ingredients. Adjust to taste and set aside.

Heat the coconut oil in a wok or large frying pan over medium heat. Add the onion, garlic and chilli and stir-fry for 2 minutes or until the onion starts to soften. Add the harder vegetables (such as carrot and celery) and cook, stirring, for 2 minutes, adding a little water if needed to prevent sticking. Add the remaining vegetables and cook until just tender. Toss through the quinoa and sauce, then serve immediately, garnished with fresh herbs.

roasted beetroot salad with lentils, spinach and macadamia feta

Another partly raw/partly cooked dish that's healthy and energising. It's perfect to enjoy between seasons, and so good for you. We all know the liver loves beetroot!

SERVES 4

8 medium beetroot, peeled and cut into wedges

2 large red onions, cut into 2 cm pieces

1 tablespoon extra virgin olive oil

1 cup (200 g) brown lentils

3–4 large handfuls of baby spinach

1 red capsicum (pepper), seeds and vein removed, diced

handful of mint leaves

handful of flat-leaf parsley leaves

MACADAMIA FETA

1 cup (140 g) macadamias

1 tablespoon lemon juice

¼–½ cup (60–125 ml) filtered water

pinch of Himalayan crystal salt

PRESERVED LEMON DRESSING

1 tablespoon apple cider vinegar

1 tablespoon extra virgin olive oil

1 clove garlic, crushed

2 teaspoons raw coconut nectar

⅛ preserved lemon, (see page 156), peel only, finely diced

Preheat the oven to 180°C (350°F). Line two baking trays with baking paper.

Place the beetroot on one tray and roast for 30–60 minutes or until soft when tested with a knife or skewer. When the beetroot has been cooking for 15 minutes, place the onion on the second tray, drizzle with the olive oil and roast for 25 minutes or until just starting to colour. Remove and allow to cool slightly.

Meanwhile, cook the lentils according to the packet instructions. Drain.

To prepare the feta, place all the ingredients in a high-powered blender or food processor and blend until combined.

To make the dressing, place all the ingredients in a glass jar and shake to combine. Adjust to taste.

Place the beetroot, onion, lentils, spinach, capsicum and herbs in a large bowl, add the dressing and gently toss to combine. Serve topped with macadamia feta.

sna

chapter

5

spicy seed mix

Scatter a handful of this spicy mix over a salad for crunch and flavour, or enjoy on its own as a healthy snack. I always keep a constant supply of this in my pantry.

**MAKES ABOUT 4 CUPS
(600 G)**

1 teaspoon Himalayan crystal salt

1 clove garlic, very finely grated

1 teaspoon onion powder

1 teaspoon smoked paprika

1 teaspoon chilli powder

pinch of cayenne pepper

splash of tamari

1 tablespoon raw honey

1 tablespoon lemon juice

2 cups (300 g) sunflower seeds, soaked for 4 hours in filtered water, then rinsed and drained

1 cup (140 g) pumpkin seeds, soaked for 4 hours in filtered water, then rinsed and drained

1 cup (150 g) sesame seeds

Mix together the salt, garlic, onion powder, paprika, chilli powder, cayenne pepper, tamari, honey and lemon juice in a large bowl. Adjust to taste. Add the sunflower, pumpkin and sesame seeds and stir to coat.

Spread out the mixture on dehydrator trays lined with baking paper or paraflexx sheets and dehydrate at 43°C (110°F) for 24 hours or until dry. Store in airtight glass jars in the pantry for up to 3 months.

corn chips

Inspired by a recipe by Chad Sarno, these delicious crackers are great for serving with spicy Mexican-style food (see page 136) or as a base for your favourite toppings.

MAKES ABOUT 60

8 corn cobs, kernels removed

1 cup (140 g) macadamias, soaked for 2 hours in filtered water, then rinsed and drained

¾ cup (75 g) whole golden flaxseeds or linseeds, soaked overnight in filtered water (just enough to cover)

pinch of chilli powder

1 tablespoon dried coriander

pinch of cayenne pepper

1 tablespoon onion powder

1 teaspoon garlic powder

1 teaspoon Himalayan crystal salt

Combine all the ingredients in a food processor and blend until smooth. Pour the mixture onto dehydrator trays lined with baking paper or paraflexx sheets and work it out to the edges, ensuring the mixture is an even thickness (about 2–3 mm).

Dehydrate at 63°C (145°F) for 1 hour, then score with a cranked-handled spatula to your desired size and shape. Reduce the temperature to 43°C (110°F) and dehydrate for about 8 hours. Flip the corn chips after this time, then continue to dehydrate until they are crispy (should take another 8 hours).

Break along the score lines and store in airtight containers, ready to serve with your favourite dip or Mexican dish!

cheese plate with preserved lemons, inca jam and turmeric pickle

Use the preserved lemons to ramp up the flavour in salads, pasta dishes, cheese and crackers or anything that you want to add extra zing to. Inca berries have a wonderful tart flavour that pairs well with cheese and crackers – the inca jam here is like a quince paste. The pickle is a nice accompaniment to cheese, salads, crackers and canapes.

SERVES 6

fermented nut cheese (see page 207) and your choice of bread or crackers, to serve

PRESERVED LEMONS
6 large lemons, quartered
½ cup (60 g) mineral salt
1 long green chilli, seeded and roughly chopped
2 cloves garlic
1 brown onion, roughly chopped
2 bay leaves
lemon juice, to cover

INCA JAM
1 cup (130 g) inca berries, soaked in filtered water for a few hours until softened, drained
¾ cup (150 g) Irish moss paste (see page 26)
2 tablespoons white chia seeds
¼ cup (60 ml) apple cider vinegar
¾ cup (105 g) coconut sugar
½ teaspoon Himalayan crystal salt, or to taste

TURMERIC PICKLE
2 teaspoons fenugreek seeds
2 teaspoons mustard seeds
¾ cup (150 g) finely chopped turmeric root
1 teaspoon mustard powder

1 teaspoon ground ginger
pinch of cayenne pepper
½ cup (125 ml) lime juice
¼ cup (60 ml) olive oil, plus extra for sealing the jar
1 teaspoon mineral salt
finely grated zest of 1 lime
1 tablespoon white miso paste
2 tablespoons coconut sugar
1 green capsicum (pepper), seeds and vein removed, finely diced
1 tablespoon grated ginger

To make the preserved lemons, place the lemon quarters in a large bowl. Add the salt and use your hands to rub the salt into the lemons. Place the lemons, chilli, garlic, onion and bay leaves in a sterilised 1 litre jar (or use smaller jars) and pack down tightly with a tamper or wooden rolling pin. Pour in enough lemon juice to cover the ingredients.

Seal the jar with a lid and leave to sit at room temperature out of direct sunlight for 1 month, turning the jar from time to time.

Make sure the contents remain completely covered with lemon juice – keep a dish under the jar to catch any juices that may bubble over. After 1 month transfer the lemons to the fridge, where they will keep indefinitely. Makes about 1 litre.

For the inca jam, place all the ingredients in a high-powered blender and blend well. Adjust to taste. Pour into a container or jar with a lid and place in the fridge to set overnight. It will keep in the fridge for up to 3 weeks. Makes 1½ cups (480 g).

To make the pickle, gently heat a frying pan, add the fenugreek and mustard seeds and roast until fragrant. Remove from the pan and allow to cool, then finely grind with a mortar and pestle. Combine all the ingredients in a bowl and adjust to taste.

Spoon the pickle into small sterilised jars and seal with extra olive oil. Store in the fridge for up to 12 months – the longer the pickle is kept the better it tastes! Makes about 2 cups (560 g).

Serve the preserved lemon, inca jam and pickle with fermented nut cheese and your choice of bread or crackers.

crunchy seed crackers

I always have a stash of these versatile crackers in my pantry as they go well with just about everything. Serve them with your favourite cheese, dip, salsa or salad. This makes a large batch, which is super handy as they have a long shelf life.

MAKES ABOUT 60

2 cups (280 g) whole golden flaxseeds or linseeds

1 cup (150 g) sunflower seeds

1 cup (140 g) pumpkin seeds

½ cup (60 g) chia seeds

½ cup (150 g) sesame seeds

3 cups (750 ml) filtered water

1 bunch flat-leaf parsley

1 bunch coriander

1 onion, roughly chopped

1 clove garlic

1 red capsicum (pepper), seeds and vein removed, roughly chopped

1 teaspoon mineral salt

1 teaspoon dried oregano

1 teaspoon ground ginger

1 teaspoon coriander seeds,

¼ teaspoon smoked paprika

pinch of cayenne pepper

2 tablespoons apple cider vinegar

1 teaspoon onion powder

2 zucchini (courgettes), peeled and roughly chopped

⅓ cup (80 ml) raw coconut nectar

Combine all the seeds in a large bowl, add the water and leave to soak for 8 hours or overnight. Do not drain the water from this mix once soaked as you will notice it has become gelatinous. This will help hold the crackers together.

Blend together the remaining ingredients and stir into the seed mixture. Adjust to taste.

Spread out the mixture on dehydrator trays lined with baking paper or paraflexx sheets, ensuring the mixture is an even thickness (2–3 mm). Score with a crank-handled spatula to your desired size and shape. Dehydrate at 43°C (110°F) for 8 hours, then flip the mixture over if the top is dry. Dehydrate for a further 24 hours or until crispy. Break along the score lines and store in airtight containers for up to 3 months.

kale and coconut chips

These are seriously addictive but oh so good for you. As well as tasting good, kale has powerful antioxidants, and is high in calcium.

MAKES ABOUT 200 G

2 bunches kale, stems removed, leaves torn into large bite-sized pieces
1 cup (50 g) coconut flakes

MARINADE
½ cup (140 g) tahini
2 tablespoons extra virgin olive oil
few drops of stevia liquid
1 teaspoon Himalayan crystal salt
juice of 1 lemon
¼ cup (60 ml) tamari
1 clove garlic, finely grated
1 teaspoon ground coriander
2 teaspoons sesame oil
pinch of cayenne pepper

To make the marinade, blend all the ingredients together.

Pour the marinade over the torn kale and massage into the leaves. Stir through the coconut flakes. Adjust to taste.

Spread out the kale mixture on dehydrator trays lined with baking paper or paraflexx sheets. Dehydrate at 40°C (105°F) for 6–8 hours or until crisp. Flip the trays halfway through the dehydrating time. Store the chips in an airtight container in the pantry for up to 3–4 weeks.

Note

You may need to stop the kale chips from moving around due to the fan in the dehydrator. You can do this by placing a mesh screen from another dehydrator tray over them.

green hazelnut cherry power bars

When I was playing around with this recipe while in Bali, I discovered that hazelnuts, cherries and spirulina are a match made in heaven! Inspired by Elaina Love, this great recipe combines all of these fabulous ingredients.

MAKES 16

2 cups (280 g) hazelnuts, soaked for 2–4 hours in filtered water, then rinsed and drained

1 cup (160 g) brazil nuts

1 cup (150 g) cashews

¼ cup (25 g) spirulina powder

⅓ cup (35 g) cacao powder

¼ cup (20 g) shredded coconut

⅓ cup (40 g) chia seeds

2 tablespoons coconut oil, melted

½ cup (100 g) powdered xylitol

15 drops of cherry extract

2 teaspoons vanilla extract

pinch of mineral salt

¼ cup (60 ml) filtered water, plus extra if needed

¼ cup (35 g) pitted medjool dates

½ cup (90 g) dried sour cherries

Spread out the hazelnuts on a dehydrator tray lined with baking paper or paraflexx sheets and dehydrate at 40°C (105°F) for 6 hours.

Line a 28 cm × 18 cm slice tin with baking paper.

Place the nuts in a food processor and pulse until finely chopped. Add the spirulina, cacao, coconut, chia seeds, coconut oil, xylitol powder, cherry extract, vanilla extract and a pinch of salt and process until a dough forms, adding the water gradually if needed. Add the dates and cherries and pulse until coarsely chopped.

Press the mixture into the prepared tin and refrigerate for several hours or until set. Cut into bars to serve.

ginger goji maca cookies

These superfood cookies are a delicious guilt-free treat, and if you decorate them with chocolate sauce they are irresistible! Store and serve from the freezer for added crunch. To make your own coconut flour simply blend shredded coconut in a blender.

MAKES 25–40,
DEPENDING ON SIZE

1 tablespoon grated ginger

½ cup (85 g) coconut flour
(see recipe introduction)

2 tablespoons whole flaxseeds

2 tablespoons chia seeds

1 tablespoon hemp protein powder
(or other vegan/sugar-free protein
powder)

1 tablespoon maca powder

1 tablespoon lucuma powder

1 teaspoon vanilla extract

2 tablespoons coconut oil, melted

1 cup (200 g) powdered xylitol

1 cup (150 g) sesame seeds

1 cup (150 g) sunflower seeds

1 teaspoon ground cinnamon

pinch of ground cardamom

½ cup (70 g) pitted medjool dates

¾ cup (150 g) Irish moss paste
(see page 26)

pinch of Himalayan crystal salt

2 cups (240 g) almond meal

¼ cup (25 g) goji berries

filtered water, to bind (if needed)

chocolate sauce (see page 209),
to decorate (optional)

Place all the ingredients except the almond meal, goji berries, water and chocolate sauce in a food processor and blitz to form a paste. Transfer to a bowl. Add the almond meal and goji berries and mix well with your hands, adding enough water to bind to a dough consistency.

Scoop out the dough using a small ice-cream scoop, melon baller or spoon and dollop onto dehydrater trays lined with baking paper or paraflexx sheets. Flatten with a fork to create a cookie shape.

Dehydrate at 40°C (105°F) for about 24 hours. For extra yumminess, you can decorate the cookies with a dollop of chocolate sauce and place in the freezer to set.

naughty but nice bliss balls

These are great to make as little treats to take to your friends, or keep them at work for when the munchies strike!

MAKES ABOUT 25

200 g nuts (brazil nuts or cashews), soaked for 2 hours in filtered water, then rinsed and drained

2 tablespoons sunflower seeds, soaked for 4 hours in filtered water, then rinsed and drained

350 g dried fruit (medjool dates, apricots, prunes), pitted

1 tablespoon chia seeds

2 tablespoons almond butter

2 tablespoons cacao powder

1 tablespoon raw coconut nectar

1 tablespoon coconut oil, melted

2 teaspoons maca powder

½ teaspoon ground cinnamon

shredded coconut, for rolling

Spread out the nuts and sunflower seeds on a dehydrator tray lined with baking paper or paraflexx sheets. Dehydrate at 43°C (110°F) for 24 hours.

Place the nuts and sunflower seeds in a food processor and process until coarsely chopped. Add the dried fruit and process until finely chopped and the mixture forms a coarse paste. Add the remaining ingredients (except the shredded coconut) and pulse to combine.

Take 1 tablespoon of mixture at a time and roll into balls, moistening your hands with water if necessary. Roll in shredded coconut to coat.

Store the balls in the fridge for up to 2 weeks.

choc-orange bliss balls

A nut-free version of bliss balls – perfect to pack into the kids' lunchboxes.

MAKES 20

1⅓ cups (200 g) sunflower seeds, soaked for 4 hours in filtered water, then rinsed and drained

1¼ cups (175 g) pitted medjool dates

2 tablespoons desiccated coconut

2 tablespoons cacao powder, plus extra for rolling

1 teaspoon vanilla extract

finely grated zest of 2 oranges

few drops of orange oil or 1 teaspoon orange flower water (or to taste)

1½ tablespoons coconut oil, melted

2–3 tablespoons orange juice

2 tablespoons cacao nibs

Spread out the sunflower seeds on a dehydrator tray lined with baking paper or paraflexx sheets. Dehydrate at 43°C (110°F) for 12–24 hours.

Place the sunflower seeds in a food processor and process until finely chopped. Add the dates and coconut and process until finely chopped. Add the cacao powder, vanilla, orange zest, orange oil or orange flower water and coconut oil and process to a paste, adding just enough orange juice to bind the mixture together. Add the cacao nibs and pulse briefly to distribute through the mixture.

Take 1 tablespoon of mixture at a time and roll into balls, moistening your hands with water if necessary. Roll in extra cacao powder to coat.

Store the bliss balls in the fridge for up to 2 weeks, or in the freezer indefinitely!

6

chapter

dess

apple cinnamon superfood cake with apricot glaze

This cake is not only loaded with superfoods, it's a great way to use up leftover almond pulp from making nut milk (see page 204). You can also use any nut pulp – it doesn't have to be almonds, or almond meal is fine too. Enjoy this lovely treat for afternoon tea with a dollop of whipped cream and a dusting of cinnamon. For added texture, you could also top with a handful of crumbly crunch topping (see page 74).

SERVES 8-12

2 granny smith apples, peeled, cored and finely chopped

2 cups (180 g) almond pulp (see recipe introduction)

½ cup (80 g) currants, soaked for 30 minutes in hot water, drained and rinsed

2 teaspoons ground cinnamon, plus extra for dusting

pinch of Himalayan crystal salt

2 teaspoons maca powder

2 teaspoons lucuma powder

1 teaspoon mixed spice

2 tablespoons psyllium husk powder

1 cup (110 g) roughly chopped walnuts

2 ripe avocados, peeled, stones removed

⅔ cup (140 g) coconut oil, melted

⅓ cup (120 g) manuka honey

6 squirts of stevia liquid, or to taste

½ granny smith apple, extra, thinly sliced

whipped cream (see page 208), to serve

APRICOT GLAZE

3-4 dried apricots, soaked until soft, then rinsed and drained

juice of 1 lemon

⅓ cup (80 ml) filtered water

3 squirts of stevia liquid, or to taste

pinch of Himalayan crystal salt

To make the apricot glaze, place all the ingredients in a small high-powered blender and blend until smooth. Set aside.

Combine the chopped apple, almond pulp, currants, cinnamon, salt, maca powder, lucuma powder, mixed spice, psyllium husk powder and walnuts in a large bowl.

Put the avocados, coconut oil, honey and stevia in a high-powered blender and whiz until smooth. Adjust to taste. Add to the bowl with the other ingredients and stir to combine.

Pour the batter into a lined 23 cm round tin with a removable base and press down firmly. Arrange the apple slices over the top and brush with apricot glaze (this will give the cake a 'cooked' appearance and a nice sweet finish).

At this point you can place the cake in the freezer for a few hours, then store it in the fridge until needed. If you wish the cake to have a drier finish, and really look and taste like cake, dehydrate it – just transfer the cake to a plate and dehydrate at 73°C (165°F) for 2 hours, then reduce the temperature to 43°C (110°F) and dehydrate for a further 8–10 hours. Brush with any remaining apricot glaze during the dehydrating time if desired.

Dust the cake with cinnamon and serve with whipped cream.

raspberry and almond chunk choc mousse cheesecake

This recipe is a further development of my firm favourite, choc mousse cheesecake. I always have this one on hand in the freezer for when unexpected guests turn up, and everyone loves it!

SERVES 8

chocolate sauce (see page 209), shredded coconut, crushed freeze-dried raspberries and goji berries, to serve

BASE

1 cup (160 g) almonds

1 cup (160 g) currants

¼ cup (20 g) desiccated coconut

⅓ cup (70 g) coconut oil, melted

1 full dropper of medicine flowers dark chocolate extract or 1 tablespoon cacao powder

pinch of Himalayan crystal salt

FILLING

1½ cups (225 g) cashews, soaked for 1 hour in filtered water, then rinsed and drained

½ cup (50 g) cacao powder

2 tablespoons cacao butter, melted

¼ cup (50 g) coconut oil, melted

⅔ cup (160 ml) raw coconut nectar

¼ cup (50 g) Irish moss paste (see page 26) or coconut oil, melted

pinch of Himalayan crystal salt

1 teaspoon vanilla extract or 1 full dropper of medicine flowers vanilla extract

filtered water (optional)

1 cup (30 g) freeze-dried raspberries (or any berries you like), lightly crushed

½ cup (80 g) roughly chopped almonds

To make the base, spread out the almonds on a dehydrator tray lined with baking paper or paraflexx sheets. Dehydrate at 43°C (110°F) for 24 hours. Blitz all the ingredients in a food processor until crumbly. Press into a 20 cm springform tin and leave in the fridge while you make the filling

For the filling, blend all the ingredients except the raspberries and almonds in a high-powered blender until smooth. Add a little water if the mixture is too thick. Stir in the raspberries and almonds by hand. Pour evenly over the base, then place in the freezer for 2–3 hours or until set. Transfer to the fridge for 30 minutes before serving.

Drizzle chocolate sauce over the top and decorate with shredded coconut, freeze-dried raspberries and goji berries. Serve.

raw pecan pie

This amazing pie is decadent and addictive. Pecan and caramel are a match made in heaven; combine that with cream and you have utter perfection. Make your own coconut flour by blending shredded coconut into a powder – great for the budget conscious!

SERVES 8–12

PECAN TOPPING

1½ cups (180 g) pecans, soaked for 4 hours in filtered water, then rinsed and drained

½ cup (70 g) coconut sugar

2 tablespoons maple syrup

1 teaspoon ground cinnamon

½ teaspoon Himalayan crystal salt

¼ teaspoon ground nutmeg

½ teaspoon mixed spice

¼ teaspoon ground ginger

¼ teaspoon ground star anise

MACADAMIA BASE

1½ cups (210 g) macadamias

1 cup (170 g) coconut flour (see recipe introduction)

¼ cup (50 g) powdered xylitol

1 teaspoon vanilla extract or 10 drops of medicine flowers vanilla extract

¼ cup (50 g) coconut oil, melted

pinch of Himalayan crystal salt

CARAMEL LAYER

⅓ cup (95 g) raw almond butter

¾ cup (180 g) date paste (made by blending pitted medjool dates with just enough filtered water to make a thick paste)

¾ cup (185 ml) raw coconut nectar

1 teasoon vanilla extract

pinch of Himalayan crystal salt

CREAM LAYER

1 cup (160 g) young coconut flesh (from 1–2 coconuts)

½ cup (75 g) cashews, soaked for 2 hours in filtered water, then rinsed and drained

16 drops of medicine flowers peanut extract

1 tablespoon raw coconut nectar

¼ cup (60 ml) coconut water (or filtered water), plus extra if needed

To prepare the pecan topping, combine all the ingredients in a bowl. Spread out the mixture on a dehydrator tray lined with baking paper or paraflexx sheets and dehydrate at 40°C (105°F) for 24 hours.

For the base, place all the ingredients in a food processor and blitz until combined and holding together. Press into the base and side of a 23 cm fluted tin with a removable base and place in the freezer while you make the caramel layer.

To make the caramel layer, combine all the ingredients in a high-powered blender or food processor and blend until smooth. Spread over the macadamia base and place in the fridge.

For the cream layer, place all the ingredients in a high-powered blender or food processor and blend until smooth and the consistency of thick cream (adjust with a little more liquid if necessary).

Spread the cream layer over the caramel layer, then place a layer of the prepared pecans on top. Chop any remaining pecans and reserve to sprinkle over for serving. Return to the fridge for 2-3 hours to set, then serve, sprinkled with chopped pecans.

salted caramel buck nut clusters

The ideal sweet treat to have on hand for when the cravings strike – with no guilt. These are seriously addictive and get gobbled up in no time at home. Sprouted buckwheat is super alkalising, and cacao powder is rich in iron.

MAKES 25

¼ cup (25 g) walnuts, soaked for 4 hours in filtered water, then rinsed, drained and roughly chopped

¼ cup (35 g) pumpkin seeds, soaked for 4–6 hours in filtered water, then rinsed and drained

¼ cup (35 g) sesame seeds, soaked for 4 hours in filtered water, then rinsed and drained

½ cup (50 g) sprouted buckwheat (see page 40)

¾ cup (150 g) coconut oil, melted

½ cup (50 g) cacao powder

1 cup (75 g) shredded coconut

⅓ cup (45 g) cacao nibs

⅓ cup (35 g) goji berries

⅓ cup (50 g) raisins

½ teaspoon Himalayan crystal salt, or to taste

12–15 drops of medicine flowers caramel extract, to taste, or 1 tablespoon mesquite powder

¼ cup (25 g) powdered xylitol

½ quantity chocolate sauce (see page 209), still liquid, to coat

Spread out the walnuts, pumpkin seeds and sesame seeds on a dehydrator tray lined with baking paper or paraflexx sheets and dehydrate at 43°C (110°F) for 24 hours.

Spread out the sprouted buckwheat on a dehydrator tray lined with baking paper or paraflexx sheets and dehydrate at 43°C (110°F) for 8–12 hours or until dried.

Place the buckwheat, walnuts and seeds in a large bowl, add all the remaining ingredients except the chocolate sauce and stir to combine. Adjust to taste – you want a nice salty caramel flavour coming through. Allow to thicken slightly, then drop spoonfuls of the mixture into mini muffin holes and pop in the freezer for 30 minutes or until set.

Remove the clusters from the muffin tray and dip into the chocolate sauce to coat. Place on a baking tray lined with baking paper and return to the freezer to set. Eat them straight from the freezer.

Note

For a low-sugar or sugar-free option, omit the raisins and goji berries.

date scones with vanilla bean butter

This one is for my Dad – he loves scones, but not the healthy ones. I'm hoping this recipe will convert him! If you don't have almond pulp left over from making nut milk you can use any other nut pulp, almond meal or process 1 cup (160 g) almonds to fine breadcrumbs in a food processor.

MAKES 9

1 cup (90 g) psyllium husks

2 cups (180 g) almond pulp
(see recipe introduction)

3 teaspoons mixed spice

3 teaspoons ground cinnamon

1 teaspoon vanilla bean powder or
vanilla extract

1½ cups (210 g) pitted medjool dates,
roughly chopped

½ cup (50 g) flaxseed meal

finely grated zest of 1 lemon

3 drops of 100% pure organic
essential oil of lemon (optional)

1 teaspoon Himalayan crystal salt

1 cup (250 ml) filtered water, plus
extra if needed

VANILLA BEAN BUTTER

2 cups (400 g) coconut oil, melted

⅓ cup (80 ml) raw coconut nectar
(or raw honey or powdered xylitol)

large pinch of mineral salt (or to taste)

2 vanilla beans, seeds scraped

8 drops of medicine flowers
vanilla extract

⅛–¼ teaspoon ground turmeric

Place all the ingredients except the water in a bowl and stir to combine. Gradually add the water and work the ingredients with your hands until you reach a dough consistency. Tip out the dough onto a sheet of baking paper and press out to a thickness of about 3–4 cm. Cut into nine squares.

Place the scones on a dehydrator tray lined with baking paper or paraflexx sheets. Dehydrate at 54°C (130°F) for 1 hour, then reduce the temperature to 43°C (110°F) and dehydrate for 6–8 hours or until dry.

To make the vanilla bean butter, place all the ingredients in a blender and blend until combined. Store in the fridge for up to 3 weeks. To soften, leave the butter out on the bench for 30 minutes or gently warm it in a dehydrator at 35°C (95°F) for 10 minutes. Stir to fluff up the butter and serve.

Serve the scones gently warmed from the dehydrator, spread generously with the vanilla bean butter.

vanilla coconut macadamia ice-cream with chocolate sauce

I can't eat traditional ice-cream thanks to the refined sugar and lactose from the dairy. So I am thrilled with this: a healthy, guilt-free ice-cream with no side-effects!

MAKES 1 LITRE

2 cups (500 ml) almond milk
(see page 204)

2 cups (320 g) young coconut flesh
(from about 2 coconuts)

1½ cups (210 g) macadamias, soaked
for 2 hours in filtered water, then
rinsed and drained

2 teaspoons psyllium husk powder

1 cup (200 g) powdered xylitol

¼ cup (50 g) coconut oil, melted

2 vanilla beans, seeds scraped

1 teaspoon vanilla essence or 16 drops
of medicine flowers vanilla extract

¼ cup (50 g) Irish moss paste
(see page 26)

pinch of Himalayan crystal salt

chocolate sauce (see page 209),
to serve

Place the almond milk, coconut flesh and macadamias in a high-powered blender and blend until creamy. Add the remaining ingredients except the chocolate sauce and blend until smooth, adjusting the flavour to taste (make it a little sweeter than normal as freezing will slightly reduce the sweetness). Pour into a container, cover with a lid and freeze overnight.

Serve the ice-cream with the chocolate sauce. It will set like chocolate crackle when it hits the ice-cream!.

rocky road chocolate slab

The marshmallow needs to be made ahead of time so it can set in the freezer before you make balls of it to coat in chocolate. You may not need all the marshmallow in the slab, but I generally find having a little left over is no problem – it always gets eaten. For a party, triple the recipe and make some mega slabs!

SERVES ABOUT 20

¼ cup (25 g) goji berries

¼ cup (30 g) inca berries

½ cup (70 g) chopped mixed nuts (such as hazelnuts, pecans or almonds)

MARSHMALLOW

½ cup (75 g) raw cashews, soaked for 2 hours in filtered water, then rinsed and drained

½ cup (80 g) young coconut flesh (from about ½ coconut)

½ cup (100 g) Irish moss paste (see page 26) (optional)

¼ cup (60 ml) coconut water

½ cup (100 g) powdered xylitol

⅓ cup (70 g) coconut oil, melted

2 tablespoons coconut butter

1 vanilla bean, seeds scraped

1 teaspoon vanilla extract

pinch of Himalayan crystal salt

CHOCOLATE

¼ cup (35 g) cacao powder

¼ cup (60 ml) raw coconut nectar

¼ cup (50 g) coconut oil, melted

2 tablespoons grated cacao butter

1 teaspoon lemon juice

1 teaspoon vanilla extract

pinch of Himalayan crystal salt

To prepare the marshmallow, combine all the ingredients in a high-powered blender and blend until smooth. Pour into a small tray or a muffin tray and place in the freezer for about 2 hours to set.

To make the chocolate, place all the ingredients in a heatproof bowl set over a saucepan of barely simmering water and stir until smooth and combined. Remove from the heat and allow to cool slightly.

Once the marshmallow has set, use a spoon or small melon baller to create small balls. Drop the balls in the cooled chocolate to coat. Transfer to a baking tray lined with baking paper and place in the freezer to set.

Line a 27 cm × 8 cm bar tin or a tray with baking paper. Combine the berries, nuts, chocolate and marshmallow in a bowl, working quickly so the marshmallow doesn't melt. Pour the mixture into the prepared tin and immediately place in the freezer for 2 hours to set. Once set, cut into chunks and enjoy at your leisure!

key lime slice with lime cream and raspberries

This is a wonderfully light dish, courtesy of the coconut filling and fresh lime. A great summer dessert to share with friends.

SERVES 8

fresh raspberries, to serve
mint leaves, to garnish (optional)

CRUST
1 cup (75 g) shredded coconut
2 tablespoons coconut oil, melted
1 cup (140 g) macadamias
½ cup (70 g) pitted medjool dates
pinch of Himalayan crystal salt

FILLING
2 cups (320 g) young coconut flesh (from 2–3 coconuts)
½ cup (125 ml) raw coconut nectar
½ avocado, peeled, stone removed
½ cup (100 g) coconut oil, melted
finely grated zest of 2 limes
½ cup (125 ml) lime juice
8–12 drops of medicine flowers lime extract (optional)

LIME CREAM
1 cup (150 g) cashews, soaked for 2 hours in filtered water, then rinsed and drained
½ cup (125 ml) filtered water
2 tablespoons raw coconut nectar
1 tablespoon lime juice
⅛ teaspoon vanilla extract
8–12 drops of medicine flowers lime extract (optional)

To make the crust, place the shredded coconut in a food processor and blitz until finely chopped. Add the remaining ingredients and blend until the nuts are finely chopped and the crust binds together. Press into a lined 26 cm × 16 cm slice tin or a 23 cm torte tin, then place in the fridge to chill while you make the filling.

To prepare the filling, place all the ingredients in a food processor and blend until smooth. Spoon evenly over the base, smoothing the top. Place in the fridge or freezer to set (about 2 hours in the freezer and overnight in the fridge).

To make the lime cream, place all the ingredients in a food processor and blend until smooth. Transfer to a squeezy bottle or airtight container.

Place the fresh raspberries in a zip-lock bag and crush lightly with your hands.

When ready to serve, remove the slice from the fridge or freezer (if it was in the freezer do this 30 minutes before serving). Slice into squares. Decorate the slice with smashed raspberries and some of their juices, and serve with the lime cream on the side or squeeze it over the top in a zig-zag pattern. Garnish with fresh mint, if desired.

turkish delight choc chia pudding

I love Turkish delight, and I'm thrilled that this recipe offers all the flavour without all the sugar. Chia seeds help detoxify the body and are full of minerals, protein and essential fatty acids. While this makes a beautiful dessert, it may also be enjoyed as a decadent breakfast.

SERVES 4

1½ cups (375 ml) almond milk (see page 204)

½ avocado, peeled, seeded

¼ cup (60 ml) raw coconut nectar

2 tablespoons cacao powder

pinch of Himalayan crystal salt

¼ cup (30 g) chia seeds

½ cup (90 g) pomegranate seeds, plus extra to serve

¼ cup (70 g) shelled pistachios, plus extra, roughly chopped, to serve

2–3 teaspoons rosewater or 8–12 drops of medicine flowers rose extract

1 teaspoon vanilla extract or 8–10 drops of medicine flowers vanilla extract

filtered water, if needed

mint sprigs or rose petals, to garnish (optional)

Place the almond milk, avocado, coconut nectar, cacao powder and salt in a high-powered blender and blend until smooth.

Place the chia seeds in a bowl, pour the milk mixture over the top and stir to combine. Add the remaining ingredients except the water and garnishes, then pour into four serving dishes and refrigerate overnight to set. Add a little water if the mixture is too thick.

Scatter extra pomegranate seeds and pistachios over the top and serve garnished with mint sprigs or rose petals, if liked.

Note

To make this sugar free, omit the coconut nectar and replace with ¼ cup (50 g) powdered xylitol and 3–6 drops of stevia liquid.

carrot muffins with orange cashew cream

This is a bit of a twist on carrot cake, in muffin form for healthy snacking, and can also double as a healthy breakfast too. You can use the leftover almond pulp from making almond milk (see page 204) instead of the almond meal, if preferred.

MAKES 10

2 cups (240 g) almond meal

2 tablespoons chia seeds

½ cup (70 g) pitted medjool dates

1 cup (80 g) desiccated coconut

½ cup (125 ml) raw coconut nectar

finely grated zest of 1 orange

1 teaspoon ground cinnamon, plus extra to garnish (optional)

¼ teaspoon ground nutmeg

¼ teaspoon ground ginger

pinch of Himalayan crystal salt

1 teaspoon vanilla extract

pinch of mineral salt

2 cups (230 g) grated carrot

1 cup (100 g) walnuts, roughly chopped, plus extra to garnish

ORANGE CASHEW CREAM

1 cup (150 g) cashews, soaked for 2 hours in filtered water, then rinsed and drained

¼ cup (50 g) coconut oil, melted

¼ cup (60 ml) orange juice

¼ cup (50 g) powdered xylitol

1½ tablespoons lemon juice

½ teaspoon vanilla extract

pinch of mineral salt

Line 10 × ⅓ cup (80 ml) muffin holes with paper cases.

Place all the ingredients except the carrot and walnuts in a food processor and blend until smooth. Add the carrot and pulse just to combine – you want the carrot to be chopped but still visible. Stir in the walnuts, then spoon into the paper cases and smooth the top. Refrigerate while you make the orange cream.

To prepare the cream, combine all the ingredients in a food processor and blend until smooth. If necessary, chill until it reaches the consistency of thick cream, then spread over the muffins. Return to the fridge until you are ready to serve – the muffins will firm up as they chill. Scatter with extra chopped walnuts and dust with extra cinnamon, if liked.

ice blocks

These are a great treat to have in the freezer for the little kids and big kids alike! They also make a quick and easy dessert, free of dairy and refined sugar. You can buy ice-block moulds from most good kitchen stores and online, otherwise just use cut-off paper cups.

SERVES 4

YOGHURT FRUIT ICE BLOCKS

1 cup (280 g) coconut yoghurt (see page 212), sweetened to taste with stevia liquid

½ cup (120 g) pureed fruit (such as strawberry, raspberry or passionfruit)

2 teaspoons raw coconut nectar, or to taste

pinch of mineral salt

Place the coconut yoghurt in a bowl. Mix together the pureed fruit, coconut nectar and salt, then add to the yoghurt and stir gently to create swirls. Spoon into ice-block moulds and freeze for 3–4 hours or until set.

SERVES 4

MANGO ICE BLOCKS

1 mango, peeled, stone removed

½ cup (125 ml) nut milk (see page 204) or coconut milk

2 teaspoons lime juice

squirt of stevia liquid

pinch of mineral salt

Place all the ingredients in a food processor and blend until smooth and well combined. Adjust to taste. Spoon into ice-block moulds and freeze for 3–4 hours or until set.

SERVES 4

CHOC BANANA ICE-CREAM

2 frozen bananas, broken into chunks

1 tablespoon almond butter

2 medjool dates, pitted

2 teaspoons cacao powder

pinch of mineral salt

½ teaspoon vanilla extract

2 teaspoons cacao nibs

Place the banana in a food processor and process in bursts until finely chopped. Add the almond butter, dates, cacao powder, salt and vanilla and blend until smooth and creamy. Lastly, add the cacao nibs and pulse briefly to just combine. Eat immediately or freeze in ice-block moulds.

mango parfait with star anise, coconut and walnuts

Mango and star anise together are just divine. Add the creaminess of coconut and the crunch of walnuts and you have a truly wonderful treat.

SERVES 4

2 mangoes, peeled, stones removed

¼ teaspoon ground star anise

1–2 tablespoons lime juice

pinch of mineral salt

2 bananas

crumbly crunch topping (see page 74), chopped nuts or ground cinnamon, to serve

COCONUT AND WALNUT CREAM

flesh of 2 young coconuts, coconut water reserved

¼ cup (50 g) Irish moss paste (see page 26; optional)

½ cup (50 g) walnuts, soaked for 4 hours in filtered water, then rinsed, drained and roughly chopped

2 tablespoons powdered xylitol

1 teaspoon vanilla extract or 12–16 drops of medicine flowers vanilla extract

pinch of mineral salt

To prepare the coconut and walnut cream, place the coconut flesh in a food processor and blitz until smooth, adding as much coconut water as necessary to form a thick, creamy consistency. Add the Irish moss paste (if using) and blend again to combine. Spoon into a bowl. Stir in the remaining ingredients and set aside.

Place the mango, star anise, lime juice and salt in a food processor and blend until smooth.

Peel and dice the bananas. Divide the banana among four glass dishes and spoon the mango mixture over the top. Spoon over the coconut cream, then cover and refrigerate until you are ready to serve. Finish with a sprinkling of breakfast topping or chopped nuts or a dusting of cinnamon.

florentines

I have always loved florentines and can never say no to one (or two!) so I am delighted to be able to enjoy them again, free of refined sugar, with the added bonus of sprouted alkalising buckwheat and the healthy fats that pecans and walnuts bring to the table.

MAKES 12

¼ cup (30 g) pecans, soaked for 2–4 hours/overnight in filtered water, then rinsed, drained and roughly chopped

¼ cup (25 g) walnuts, soaked for 4–10 hours/overnight in filtered water, then rinsed, drained and roughly chopped

1 cup (100 g) sprouted buckwheat (see page 40)

½ cup (80 g) currants

¼ cup (35 g) raisins

¼ cup (25 g) goji berries

⅔ cup (160 ml) chocolate sauce (see page 209), plus extra for drizzling

½ cup (70 g) coconut sugar

1 tablespoon filtered water

Spread out the pecans and walnuts on a dehydrator tray lined with baking paper or paraflexx sheets and dehydrate at 43°C (110°F) for 24 hours.

Spread out the sprouted buckwheat on a dehydrator tray lined with baking paper or paraflexx sheets and dehydrate at 43°C (110°F) for 8–10 hours or until dry.

Combine the nuts, buckwheat and fruit in a bowl. Spoon 1 tablespoon of chocolate sauce into 12 × ⅓ cup (80 ml) silicon (or lined metal) muffin holes. Top the chocolate with the fruit and nut mixture and place in the freezer until set.

Mix the coconut sugar and water to form a thick syrupy paste and drizzle over the set nut mixture. Drizzle with extra chocolate sauce. Place in the freezer to set for about 2 hours, then store in the fridge for up to 2 weeks. They are best eaten cold from the fridge. They freeze really well also.

hazelnut layer cake

If you're looking for a decadent dessert to impress your friends with, look no further. This cake certainly has the 'wow' factor, and the hazelnuts give it such a divine flavour.

SERVES 8–10

2 cups (280 g) hazelnuts, soaked for 2–4 hours in filtered water, then rinsed and drained

¼ cup (35 g) hazelnuts, extra, soaked for 2–4 hours in filtered water, then rinsed, drained and roughly chopped

1 cup (140 g) pitted medjool dates

½ cup (50 g) cacao powder

¼ cup (60 ml) maple syrup

8–10 drops of medicine flowers peanut extract

pinch of Himalayan crystal salt

2 tablespoons cacao nibs

CHOCOLATE MOUSSE

1 large (or 1½ medium) avocado, peeled, stone removed

½ cup (125 ml) nut milk (see page 204)

½ cup (80 g) young coconut flesh (from about ½ coconut)

8–10 drops of medicine flowers dark chocolate extract (optional)

½ cup (100 g) Irish moss paste (see page 26; optional)

½ cup (100 g) powdered xylitol

6 drops of stevia liquid

¾ cup (75 g) cacao powder

⅓ cup (70 g) coconut oil, melted

1 teaspoon vanilla extract

pinch of mineral salt

Spread out the whole and chopped hazelnuts on a dehydrator tray lined with baking paper or paraflexx sheets and dehydrate at 43°C (110°F) for 24 hours.

To prepare the mousse, place the avocado, nut milk, coconut flesh, dark chocolate extract and Irish moss paste (if using) in a food processor and blend until smooth. Add the remaining ingredients and process until well combined. Set aside.

Place the whole hazelnuts in a food processor and blitz until finely chopped. Add the dates, cacao powder, maple syrup, peanut extract and salt and process to a dough-like consistency. Divide the mixture in half.

Press one portion of the hazelnut dough into a lined 20 cm springform cake tin. Top with two-thirds of the mousse.

Roll out the remaining dough between two sheets of baking paper to a round just larger than the tin. Remove the top layer of paper, place the tin on the dough and cut around it with a knife. Remove any excess dough, then place the dough circle over the tin, paper-side up. Remove the paper and gently press over the mousse. Spread over the remaining mousse and finish with a generous sprinkling of cacao nibs and extra chopped hazelnuts. Refrigerate until set, or place in the freezer if you want to speed things up – just make sure you take it out of the freezer 30 minutes before you are planning to serve it.

sugar-free peppermint chocolates

These chocolates were my go-to guilt-free sweet treat when I was healing from candida. They always satisfied the cravings but without affecting my blood sugar levels.

MAKES 12

¼ cup (25 g) cacao powder
pinch of mineral salt
¼ cup (50 g) coconut oil, melted
6–7 drops of stevia liquid
½ teaspoon vanilla essence or 10–12 drops of medicine flowers vanilla extract
¼ teaspoon peppermint essence or or 10–12 drops of medicine flowers peppermint extract

Place the cacao powder, salt and coconut oil in a heatproof bowl set over a saucepan of barely simmering water and stir until just melted. Remove the bowl from the heat.

Add the remaining ingredients and stir to combine. Adjust to taste. Pour about 1 tablespoon into your choice of chocolate mould and place in the freezer for about 20 minutes to set. Keep in the fridge or freezer for when the craving strikes!

chapter

basi

CS

N° 7

almond milk

Almond milk is another great way to get you alkaline. You can use any nut you like here – measure out the same quantity and off you go. It all tastes delicious. If you have a nut allergy, use hemp seed instead (with the added bonus of no soaking!). Hemp seeds can have quite a strong, grassy flavour so reduce the quantity to 3 tablespoons for every 1 litre of water.

MAKES ABOUT 1 LITRE

1 cup (160 g) almonds, soaked overnight in filtered water, then rinsed and drained

3 drops of stevia liquid or 1–2 pitted medjool dates

pinch of mineral salt

1 vanilla bean, seeds scraped, or 1 teaspoon vanilla extract

1 litre filtered water

Place all the ingredients in a high-powered blender and blend until well mixed. Pour through a strainer into a jug or use a nut milk bag, squeezing out any excess milk from the pulp. Don't throw away the pulp! Store it in a container in the freezer so you can use it in your baking recipes at a later date.

The nut milk is ready to enjoy straight away. Serve with a mix of your favourite nuts, chia seeds, dates and fresh berries for a delicious, nutrient-dense breakfast. It will keep in the fridge for up to 4–5 days.

cheeses:

parmesan

This is a great cheese to have on hand in the fridge to dress up your pasta or salad dishes.

MAKES ABOUT 2 CUPS
(200 G)

1 cup (155 g) pine nuts or cashews
¼ cup (15 g) nutritional yeast
2 tablespoons lemon juice
1 teaspoon mineral salt
½ teaspoon dried oregano
½ cup (125 ml) filtered water,
plus extra if needed

Place all the ingredients in a high-powered blender and blend to a thick, creamy consistency. Add a little more water if needed. Spread out the mixture in a thin layer on a dehydrator tray lined with baking paper or paraflexx sheets. Dehydrate at 40°C (105°F) for about 6 hours until dry.

Store in an airtight container in the fridge for up to 3 months. Serve sprinkled over your favourite vege pasta dishes.

ricotta

This lovely light cheese is really nice mixed through salads or simply enjoyed with crackers.

MAKES ABOUT 200 G

1 cup (140 g) macadamias
2 tablespoons nutritional yeast
juice of ½ lemon
pinch of Himalayan crystal salt
about ⅓ cup (80 ml) filtered water
(just enough to mix everything together)

Place all the ingredients in a food processor and blend until it resembles crumbly cheese. Store in an airtight container in the fridge for up to 1 week.

fermented nut cheese

Fermenting cheese not only gives it medicinal qualities thanks to the good bacteria, it also gives it a real tang that resembles a vintage cheddar cheese flavour.

MAKES 2–4 WHEELS
OF CHEESE

2 cups (280 g) macadamias or cashews, soaked for 4 hours in filtered water, then rinsed and drained

2 tablespoons pine nuts

1 cup (250 ml) filtered water

3 high-quality probiotic capsules

1 teaspoon mineral salt

2 tablespoons nutritional yeast or savoury yeast flakes

juice of ½ lemon or 2 teaspoons apple cider vinegar

your choice of dried herbs (optional)

Place the nuts, pine nuts and water in a high-powered blender and blend until smooth. Add the opened probiotic capsules and gently blend until just combined. Transfer the mixture to a colander lined with cheesecloth, then tie up the cheesecloth. Set the colander and cheese over a glass or ceramic bowl and place a weight on top, heavy enough to gently press the liquid out. Cover and culture at room temperature for 24 hours.

Once culturing is complete, transfer the cheese to a clean bowl and stir in the salt, yeast, lemon juice or vinegar and herbs (if using). Adjust to taste, then transfer to ring moulds to shape. Place in the fridge for 24 hours. The cheese is ready to serve after this time, but if you would prefer it to have a 'rind' you can dehydrate the shaped cheese. To do this, remove the ring mould and place the cheese on dehydrator tray lined with baking paper or paraflexx sheets. Dehydrate for 24 hours at 40°C (105°F). Wrap in baking paper and store in the fridge for up to 1 month.

cashew sour cream

This is a handy staple to keep in the fridge as it can also be used as a creamy salad dressing.

MAKES ABOUT 1 CUP (200 G)

1 cup (150 g) cashews, soaked for 2 hours in filtered water, then rinsed and drained

juice of 1 lemon

pinch of Himalayan crystal salt

¼–½ cup (60–125 ml) filtered water

Place the cashews, lemon juice and salt in a high-powered blender and process until smooth, gradually adding enough water to reach the desired consistency. Adjust to taste. Transfer to a bowl and store in the fridge for up to 5 days.

whipped cream

Inspired by my dear friend Elaina Love of Pure Joy Planet, this is the healthiest whipped cream recipe around! Irish moss lowers inflammation in the body, is detoxifying and strengthens the digestive system. Xylitol has a GI of 7 and does not affect candida or blood sugar.

MAKES ABOUT 500 G

⅓ cup (75 g) soaked Irish moss

1 cup (250 ml) filtered water

1 cup (200 g) powdered xylitol

½ cup (100 g) coconut oil, melted

2 tablespoons non-GMO soy lecithin powder

1 cup (160 g) young coconut flesh (from about 1 coconut)

pinch of Himalayan crystal salt

12–15 drops of vanilla essence

Blend the Irish moss and ½ cup (125 ml) water in a small high-powered blender. Add the remaining ingredients and blend until smooth. Adjust to taste.

Transfer the cream to an airtight container and place in the freezer to set overnight. Remove it from the freezer about 30 minutes before you want to use it. The cream will store in the freezer for several months.

chocolate sauce

The sauce will set after a while if you don't serve it straight away, but this is fine. When you're ready, just melt it in a heatproof bowl set over a saucepan of barely simmering water.

MAKES ABOUT
1½ CUPS (375 ML)

½ cup (50 g) cacao powder

½ cup (100 g) coconut oil, melted

½ cup (125 ml) raw coconut nectar
or raw agave

6–8 drops vanilla of medicine flowers
vanilla extract (optional)

pinch of Himalayan crystal salt

Place all the ingredients in a bowl and stir until smooth. Use straight away or store in an airtight container in your pantry for up to 1 week. Store in the fridge for up to 3 weeks.

coconut bacon

Saving the animals and cleaning up your arteries in one fell swoop! This crazy bacon tastes delicious and is great to throw into salads, sprinkle over savoury dishes, or simply enjoy as a snack on its own. If you prefer, you can use fresh shaved coconut flesh in place of the dried coconut flakes.

MAKES 2½ CUPS
(150 G)

2½ cups (125 g) large coconut flakes or shaved coconut flesh

2 tablespoons tamari

2 tablespoons liquid smoke
or 2 teaspoons smoked salt

2 tablespoons maple syrup

¼ teaspoon smoked paprika

Combine all the ingredients in a large bowl. Spread out on a dehydrator tray lined with baking paper or paraflexx sheets and dehydrate at 40°C (105°F) for 10–12 hours or until crisp. Store in an airtight container for up to 3 months.

cashew hummus

This creamy, nutritious dip is easy to digest. Enjoy with crunchy crackers (see page 158) or crudites, or put it in sandwiches for an extra burst of flavour.

**MAKES ABOUT
2 CUPS (520 G)**

2 cups (300 g) cashews soaked for 2 hours in filtered water, then rinsed and drained

⅓ cup (90 g) tahini

1 clove garlic, roughly chopped

¾ cup (185 ml) lemon juice

1 teaspoon sesame oil

1 teaspoon onion powder

1 teaspoon garlic powder

2 teaspoons ground cumin

2 teaspoons ground coriander

dash of cayenne pepper

½ cup (125 ml) olive oil, plus extra to serve

1 teaspoon Himalayan crystal salt

filtered water, if needed

1 tablespoon roughly chopped coriander (optional)

smoked paprika, to garnish

Place the cashews, tahini, garlic, lemon juice, sesame oil, onion powder, garlic powder and spices in a food processor and process well. It will retain some texture this way. If you want a completely smooth finish, try using a high-powered blender instead.

With the processor running, gradually add the olive oil, then stir in the salt and adjust to taste. Add a little water if the hummus is too thick, then stir in the coriander (if using). Dust with smoked paprika and finish with a drizzle of extra olive oil.

coconut yoghurt

This is so easy to make and a great dairy-free addition to your diet. It is literally teeming with good bacteria, but has no nasty chemical preservatives. Get in the habit of keeping a supply of this in your fridge – I always have some on hand.

MAKES ABOUT
500–750 G

2 young coconuts
1 high-quality probiotic capsule
vanilla bean powder, ground cinnamon or a few drops of stevia liquid, to flavour (optional)

Open the coconuts and pour the coconut water into a glass jar. Scoop out the flesh and trim off any hard brown shell. Place the flesh in a high-powered blender and blend with enough coconut water to bind. You can choose your desired thickness by the amount of coconut water you add.

Transfer the blended coconut to a clean mason jar and stir through the opened probiotic capsule. Leave some room at the top as the yoghurt will aerate as it cultures. Put the lid on, then cover with a tea towel and leave in a warmish place to culture for 8–24 hours – the culturing time will depend on the temperature of the room. You will know it's ready when bubbles have formed through the yoghurt. It will become sourer the longer you leave it.

Once you are happy with the flavour and consistency, add any flavours you like such as vanilla, cinnamon or stevia (my favourite). Or just leave it as is to use in savoury dishes. Pop the yoghurt in the fridge, where it will keep for 5–7 days.

sushi rice

This is a great filler for nori rolls (see page 98) and is delicious stirred through salads. You could also form the mixture into patties and dehydrate for mini sushi rice bites!

**MAKES 3 CUPS
(600 G)**

½ cup (75 g) sunflower seeds, soaked for 4 hours in filtered water, then rinsed and drained

½ head cauliflower, broken into florets

½ cup (75 g) cashews, soaked for 2 hours in filtered water, then rinsed and drained

1 tablespoon shiro miso paste

30 g dulse flakes

2 tablespoons apple cider vinegar

⅓ cup (80 ml) coconut nectar

¼ teaspoon mineral salt

1½ tablespoons tamari

3 drops of stevia liquid

1 tablespoon olive oil

¼ cup (60 ml) filtered water, or more if needed

3 tablespoons chopped chives

1 tablespoon chopped dill

2 sticks celery, finely diced

Spread out the sunflower seeds on a dehydrator tray lined with baking paper or paraflexx sheets. Dehydrate at 41°C (105°F) for 10–12 hours.

Blitz the cauliflower florets in a food processor until they resemble rice. Transfer to a bowl.

Place the cashews, miso, dulse flakes, vinegar, coconut nectar, salt, tamari, stevia, olive oil and water in a high-powered blender and blend until smooth. Add a little more water if necessary, but don't add too much as you want the mixture to be thick. Adjust to taste.

Add the mixture to the cauliflower rice, and stir in the sunflower seeds, chives, dill and celery. Adjust to taste and it's ready to go. Store in an airtight container in the fridge for up to 1 week.

sauerkraut

This is a an absolute 'must-have' in my fridge. Homemade sauerkraut will help with the digestion of your meal, along with providing beneficial good bacteria. Serve on crackers (see page 158), with guacamole or as a condiment to your meals. Your gut will love you for it!

MAKES ABOUT
2 LITRES

1 large head organic red cabbage
2 teaspoons Himalayan crystal salt

FLAVOURINGS (OPTIONAL)
1 green apple, finely chopped
1 carrot, grated
1 clove garlic
½ bunch kale, shredded
handful of wakame seaweed
1 tablespoon fresh or dried dill

Remove three or four outer leaves from the red cabbage and reserve. Finely chop the remaining cabbage or grate it with a mandolin into a large mixing bowl. Add the salt. Massage the cabbage with your hands or pound with rolling pin until it releases moisture. Add the flavourings (if using) and massage again.

Transfer the mixture to two clean 1 litre mason jars, pounding with a rolling pin as you go to further release the brine. Continue until you reach the shoulder of the jar, about 5 cm below the neck. Make sure the vegetables are covered by the brine as much as possible.

Now grab the reserved cabbage leaves and roll them up tightly. Place the rolls in the jars and push them down – this ensures the sauerkraut sits under the brine by 2–3 cm if possible, giving a steady start to the lacto-fermentation process.

Seal the jars with their screw-top lids, then place them on a tray to catch any liquid that may bubble over. Place in a dark spot or cover with a tea towel and leave to ferment for 3–7 days. The timing of the fermentation process depends on the temperature in the kitchen. In cooler weather the ferment will take the full 7 days, but in warmer weather it can be ready in as little as 3 days. There really is no hard-and-fast rule as the fermentation process will continue as long as it is left out at room temperature, enhancing the flavour and tang. To slow down the ferment or when you are happy with the flavour, place the jars in the fridge. The sauerkraut will keep in the fridge indefinitely.

quick and easy pesto

I love the intense flavour of pesto, and it's so versatile. Use it on your favourite pasta dish, or serve it with cheese and crackers, bread or salad.

MAKES ABOUT
1 CUP (260 G)

1 bunch basil
⅓ cup (50 g) pine nuts
⅓ cup (50 g) cashews
1 clove garlic
juice of 1 lemon
1 tablespoon nutritional yeast
¼ cup (60 ml) olive oil, plus extra if needed
1 teaspoon Himalayan crystal salt

Place all the ingredients in a high-powered blender and, using the tamper, blend on low until just combined – you still want it to have some texture. Adjust the seasoning if needed. Transfer to an airtight container and store in the fridge for up to 2–3 weeks, topped with a thin layer of olive oil.

corn burrito wraps

These will wrap anything you like for a fresh, healthy breakfast or brunch – totally gluten free and with no hidden nasties. Any leftovers may be stored in the fridge for up to 3 months.

MAKES 12

2 corn cobs, kernels removed
350 g (about 3 medium) zucchini (courgettes), peeled and roughly chopped
½ cup (45 g) psyllium husks
2 teaspoons onion powder
1 teaspoon garlic powder
¾ cup (75 g) flaxseed meal
½ teaspoon ground turmeric
pinch of cayenne pepper
½ teaspoon Himalayan crystal salt
1½ cups (375 ml) filtered water

Place the corn kernels and zucchini in a food processor and process until finely chopped. Add the dry ingredients and ½ cup (125 ml) of the water and process until smooth. Gradually add the remaining water until the mixture is the consistency of thick cream.

Spread 18 cm circles about 3 mm thick onto baking trays lined with baking paper or paraflexx sheets and dehydrate at 43°C (110°F) for approximately 4 hours, turning halfway through. When they are ready they should be dry but pliable.

cashew flatbreads

These are lovely to have as a side to soup, or make into sandwiches. I like to spread them with pesto (see facing page) and cut them into small squares – perfect to tide me over between meals.

MAKES 10

2 cups (300 g) cashews, soaked for 2 hours in filtered water, then rinsed and drained

4 sundried tomatoes, soaked for 30 minutes in filtered water, then drained

½ red onion, roughly chopped

¼ cup (20 g) psyllium husks

1 tablespoon olive oil

2 tablespoons flaxseeds, ground

1 tablespoon nutritional yeast

1 tablespoon finely chopped flat-leaf parsley

¼ teaspoon Himalayan crystal salt

1 cup (250 ml) filtered water, plus extra if needed

Place the cashews, sundried tomatoes and onion in a food processor and process until the mixture resembles breadcrumbs. Add the remaining ingredients except the water and pulse to combine. Add the water and process until the mixture forms a thick paste. Add a little extra water if it is too thick.

Spread the mixture over two dehydrator trays lined with baking paper or paraflexx sheets and score into rectangles with a knife. Dehydrate at 43°C (110°F) for 6–8 hours, turning halfway through. When the flatbreads are ready they should be dry to the touch. Store in an airtight container for up to 3 months.

herbed almond bread slices

This bread is perfect for people with gluten or wheat intolerances. Serve it with salad or soup, use it to make sandwiches, dollop with pesto or sauerkraut (see pages 216 and 214), or (my favourite) spread it with nut cheese (see page 207) topped with fresh basil, tomato and salt.

MAKES ABOUT 12

2 cups (320 g) almonds or 2 cups (180 g) almond pulp from making nut milk (see page 204)

½ cup (50 g) flaxseed meal

1 cup (90 g) psyllium husks

1 teaspoon Himalayan crystal salt

2 cloves garlic

1 onion, roughly chopped

100 g cauliflower or celeriac, roughly chopped

2 teaspoons mixed herbs, such as oregano, rosemary and thyme

juice of ½ lemon

1 tablespoon olive oil

½ cup (125 ml) filtered water, plus extra if needed

Process the almonds in a food processor until you get a chunky almond flour. Transfer to a bowl. (If you are using almond pulp ensure its thawed, then place in a bowl.) Stir in the flaxseed meal, psyllium husks and salt.

Place the garlic, onion, cauliflower or celeriac, herbs, lemon juice, olive oil and half the water in the food processor and blend to a liquid. Add to the dry ingredients and stir to combine. Pour in the remaining water and mix to make a dough, adding more water if necessary to help the dough stick together.

Spread out the dough to a thickness of about 5 mm on dehydrator trays lined with baking paper or paraflexx sheets. Dehydrate at 54°C (130°F) for 1 hour, then score into sandwich-sized squares. Reduce the temperature to 43°C (110°F) and dehydrate for 6–8 hours or until dry. Flip the squares halfway through the drying time and remove the baking paper or sheets.

Serve straight from the dehydrator while still warm. Store in plastic film and ziplock bags in the fridge for 1 month. They freeze really well too.

dressings:

Keeping a stash of homemade dressings in the fridge will really take your salads or lunches to another level. Full of flavour, they make the simplest of ingredients sing.

lemon tahini dressing

MAKES ABOUT 1½ CUPS
(375 ML)

⅓ cup (90 g) tahini

½ cup (125 ml) extra virgin olive oil

2 tablespoons nutritional yeast

1 clove garlic, crushed

⅓ cup (80 ml) apple cider vinegar

1½ tablespoons lemon juice

½ preserved lemon (see page 156), peel only, finely chopped

½ teaspoon Himalayan crystal salt

pinch of cayenne pepper

1 long red chilli, seeded and finely chopped

2 tablespoons chopped dill

Place all the ingredients in a glass jar and shake to combine. Store in the fridge for 1–2 weeks.

sweet ginger soy dressing

MAKES ABOUT 1 CUP
(250 ML)

⅓ cup (80 ml) hemp seed oil or olive oil

finely grated zest and juice of 1 lime

2 tablespoons raw coconut nectar

1 clove garlic, roughly chopped

2 pitted medjool dates or 3 drops of stevia liquid

¼ cup (60 ml) tamari

¼ cup (60 ml) sesame oil

1 tablespoon roughly chopped ginger

Place all the ingredients in a high-powered blender and blend until smooth. Adjust to taste. Store in an airtight container in the fridge for 2–3 weeks.

dressings:

sea vegetable mayonnaise

1 cup (140 g) macadamias or cashews, soaked for 2 hours in filtered water, then rinsed and drained

½ teaspoon hot English mustard

½ cup (125 ml) lemon juice

¼ cup (50 g) Irish moss paste (see page 26) or ⅓ cup (40 g) white chia seeds

1 clove garlic

1 teaspoon mineral salt

1 tablespoon apple cider vinegar

pinch of cayenne pepper

1 tablespoon dulse flakes

1 cup (250 ml) filtered water, plus extra if needed

¼ cup (60 ml) olive oil, plus extra if needed

Place all the ingredients except the water and olive oil in a high-powered blender and blend until smooth and creamy. Add the water slowly until smooth, adding a little more if the mixture is too thick, then gradually blend in the oil until combined. Adjust to taste. Store in an airtight container in the fridge for 2 weeks. This dressing also freezes well.

creamy spirulina dressing

½ cup (75 g) cashews, soaked for 2 hours in filtered water, then rinsed and drained, or ½ avocado

¼ cup (60 ml) olive oil

1 tablespoon hemp oil or olive oil

¼ cup (60 ml) apple cider vinegar

2 tablespoons raw coconut nectar

3 drops of stevia liquid

1 clove garlic

2 teaspoons spirulina powder

1 zucchini (courgette), roughly chopped

pinch of cayenne pepper

1 tablespoon white miso paste

½ cup (125 ml) filtered water, plus extra if needed

Place all the ingredients in a high-powered blender and blend until smooth, adding more water if needed to thin it down. Adjust to taste. Store in an airtight container in the fridge for up to 1 week.

quick sauces:

These sauces can go with anything. Great with spiralised veges or tossed through a salad; you can even make some of them into a soup!

creamy broccoli and avocado sauce

SERVES 4

½ cup (75 g) cashews, soaked for 2 hours in filtered water, then rinsed and drained

1 small avocado, peeled, stone removed

¼ teaspoon mineral salt, or to taste

juice of 1 lemon

handful of basil leaves, plus extra to serve

125 g broccoli, roughly chopped

2 tablespoons tahini

2 tablespoons nutritional yeast

1 teaspoon hot English mustard (optional)

1 tablespoon white miso paste

⅓ cup (80 ml) apple cider vinegar

2 tablespoons raw coconut nectar

2 cups (320 g) cherry tomatoes, halved

parmesan (see page 206), to serve (optional)

Place all the ingredients except the tomatoes and parmesan in a food processor and process to combine, leaving the sauce quite chunky. Stir through the tomatoes and serve topped with extra basil and parmesan (if using).

truffle, walnut and mushroom sauce

SERVES 4

1 cup (100 g) walnuts, soaked for 4 hours in filtered water, then rinsed and drained

½ cup (45 g) roughly chopped swiss brown mushrooms

1 tablespoon tamari

1 tablespoon truffle oil

1 tablespoon nutritional yeast

1 tablespoon white miso paste

1 clove garlic, crushed

2 tablespoons lemon juice

½ cup (125 ml) filtered water

pinch of mineral salt

parmesan (see page 206), to serve (optional)

MARINATED MUSHROOMS

100 g swiss brown mushrooms, sliced

1 tablespoon tamari

1 tablespoon extra virgin olive oil

1 bunch chives, roughly chopped

1 tablespoon roughly chopped oregano

To prepare the marinated mushrooms, combine all the ingredients in a bowl and set aside to marinate while you make the sauce.

Place all the sauce ingredients except the parmesan in a high-powered blender and blend until smooth. Adjust to taste.

Toss the marinated mushrooms through the sauce just before serving and finish with a sprinkling of parmesan, if liked.

quick sauces:

mint, coriander and lemongrass pesto

SERVES 4–6

2 bunches mint

1 bunch coriander, plus extra
to garnish

1 bunch basil

1 red chilli, seeded and roughly
chopped, plus extra to garnish

1 stem lemongrass, white part only,
roughly chopped

finely grated zest and juice of 1 lime

few drops of essential lime oil
(optional)

½ cup (75 g) cashews, plus extra,
chopped, to garnish

1 tablespoon fish sauce or tamari
(for a vegan option)

2 cloves garlic, chopped

2 cm piece of ginger, thinly sliced

2 tablespoons sesame oil

¼ cup (60 ml) extra virgin olive oil,
plus extra if needed

1 tablespoon raw coconut nectar

filtered water, if needed

lime wedges, to serve

Place all the ingredients except the
water, lime wedges and garnishes
in a high-powered blender or food
processor and blend at low speed,
adding a little water if necessary to
thin it down. Add a little more olive
oil if you need to – just make sure
the pesto is still slightly chunky.
Adjust to taste, garnish with extra
chilli, coriander and cashews and
serve with lime wedges.

marinara sauce

SERVES 4

1 cup (100 g) sundried tomatoes,
soaked overnight (if short on time,
soak for 30 minutes in hot water),
drained and roughly chopped

2 pitted medjool dates, soaked
overnight (if short on time, soak for
30 minutes in almost-boiling water).

¼ cup (60 ml) extra virgin olive oil,
plus extra if needed

¼ cup (40 g) pine nuts or cashews

⅓ cup (80 ml) apple cider vinegar

2–3 teaspoons dried Italian herbs

pinch of mineral salt, or to taste

5 vine-ripened tomatoes, seeded
and roughly chopped

handful of basil leaves, torn, plus
extra to garnish

few drops of stevia liquid (optional)

chopped olives and parmesan (see
page 206), to garnish (optional)

Place the sundried tomatoes, dates,
olive oil, nuts, vinegar, herbs and
salt in a food processor and pulse
until combined. Add the vine-
ripened tomatoes and basil and
pulse until roughly blended – you
want the sauce to have some
texture. Taste and adjust the
seasoning if necessary, and stir
in the stevia if you want a touch
more sweetness.

Serve garnished with extra
basil, olives and parmesan, if liked.

acknowledgements

Rawspiration and thanks

Mum and Dad

Karen Knowler

Lisa Wheeler – Embracing Health

David Wolfe

Tim Shaddock – Live Raw

Julie Mitsios – Earth to Table

Elaina Love – Pure Joy

Katelyn Louise

Amy Rachelle – Pure Raw

Ian Mills – Magicdust

Tara and Aaron Travers – Boda

Luciano Kross – LuX Healing

Donna Gates – Body Ecology

Belinda Kirkpatrick – Naturopath

Sandor Ellix Katz

Dr Ranga Premaratna

Dr Gabriel Cousens

All my rawmazing assistants, past and present

Andreas Moritz

Sondra Beram-Hall – The Raw Food Kitchen East

Simon Gould – Sydney Digital Marketing

All my students and clients who have embarked on their raw food
journey and are now sharing the raw love with others

Julie Gibbs and her editorial and design team at Penguin Books

The photography and recipe development team: Chris Chen, Vanessa Austin
and Grace Campbell – it was a pleasure to work with such a professional team

Bernie the pug

And thanks to everyone else I have come across on this amazing healing journey

index
recipe titles in italics

LANTERN

UK | USA | Canada | Ireland | Australia
India | New Zealand | South Africa | China

Penguin Books is part of the Penguin Random House group of companies
whose addresses can be found at global.penguinrandomhouse.com.

Penguin
Random House
Australia

First published by Penguin Group (Australia), 2015

1 3 5 7 9 10 8 6 4 2

Design by Emily O'Neill and Holly McCauley © Penguin Group (Australia)
Photography by Chris Chen
Styling by Vanessa Austin
Food preparation and recipe testing by Grace Campbell
Typeset in Archer and ITC Century by Post Pre-press Group, Brisbane, Queensland
Colour separation by Splitting Image Colour Studio, Clayton, Victoria
Printed and bound in China by RR Donnelley Asia Printing Solutions Limited

National Library of Australia
Cataloguing-in-Publication data:

Brocket, Amanda, author.
The raw food kitchen book/Amanda Brocket; Chris Chen, photographer.
ISBN: 9781921384301 (paperback)
Includes index.
Raw food diet – Recipes.
Raw foods.
Natural foods – Recipes.
Chen, Chris, photographer.

613.265

penguin.com.au/lantern

Thank you to the following stockists for their assistance in
sourcing and providing props for our photo shoot:

Brett Stone
Joss Dest Ceramics
Kim Wallace Ceramics
Mud Australia
Raw Blend
Sandy Lockwood
Excalibur Dehydrators courtesy of Zesty by Nature